BRICOLAGE

DR. SARAN S. & DONA MATHEW

Copyright © Dr. Saran S. & Dona Mathew
All Rights Reserved.

This book has been self-published with all reasonable efforts taken to make the material error-free by the author. No part of this book shall be used, reproduced in any manner whatsoever without written permission from the author, except in the case of brief quotations embodied in critical articles and reviews.

The Author of this book is solely responsible and liable for its content including but not limited to the views, representations, descriptions, statements, information, opinions and references ["Content"]. The Content of this book shall not constitute or be construed or deemed to reflect the opinion or expression of the Publisher or Editor. Neither the Publisher nor Editor endorse or approve the Content of this book or guarantee the reliability, accuracy or completeness of the Content published herein and do not make any representations or warranties of any kind, express or implied, including but not limited to the implied warranties of merchantability, fitness for a particular purpose. The Publisher and Editor shall not be liable whatsoever for any errors, omissions, whether such errors or omissions result from negligence, accident, or any other cause or claims for loss or damages of any kind, including without limitation, indirect or consequential loss or damage arising out of use, inability to use, or about the reliability, accuracy or sufficiency of the information contained in this book.

Made with ♥ on the Notion Press Platform
www.notionpress.com

Contents

Contents

Foreword

Dr. Basil Thomas
Assistant Professor, Department of English
Christian College, Chengannur, Kerala.

This endeavor by a bunch of academicians, both blooming and budding, invokes the muse in everybody's creative wisdom. The silent craftsmen behind the scenes, the editors Dr. Saran S., and Dona Mathew, played their part consummately to materialize this recording of the erudite papers from literary cognoscente. An ample illustration of the collaborative work in the field of academics happens here. The title given to the book, *Bricolage: An Introduction*, serves the purpose of this venture, as the aspirants who worked out their mettle for the successful outcome of their literary journey deserve to bear the title, bricoleur. A word of appreciation is well deserved by the team behind this book.

As the papers are from different realms of the academic areas, a multiple perspective in the approach and evaluation of a literary text is celebrated here. Post truth and multiple truths, the natural spinoff of this carnivalesque, demand the attention of the readers. The book brings to the limelight the research papers on a number of topics and research areas such as Feminism, Cartoon and Graphic Studies, Colonial stereotype, Critical Race Studies, Disability studies, Ecocriticism, Theatre and English language instruction, Cross- culturalism, Technology and English language teaching, Cultural Studies, Media, Art and cyber space, Partition studies, Identity and Diasporic Literature, War Literature, Trauma Studies, E-Commerce, etc.

This is a welcome approach from the editors as well as the writers to work on such innovative areas of academic studies that provides the enthusiastic and upcoming researchers to locate and relocate novel fields of research. I personally feel this book as a harbinger for the diversification of themes and interests which will lead to the publication of more books with such pedantic scholarship which will be an asset for the bookshelves of the erudite. I wish success to all the brains associated with this scholarly venture.

BRICOLAGE

EDIT ACADEMIC PUBLICATION

• • •

November 2022

Contributors List

1. "Elements of Modernism and Post-Modernism in the Selected Novels of Amit Chaudhuri" - *Dr. Roselin Linitta George, Assistant Professor in English, Sanpada College of Commerce and Technology, Navi Mumbai, Maharashtra.
2. "The portrayal of Bicultural Daughters and Immigrant Mothers in Amy Tan's *Two Kinds*"- *Dr. B. Muthulakshmi, Assistant Professor, Department of English, Manonmaniam Sundaranar University.
3. "The Psychology of Martyrdom in Danielle Steel's Flying Angels" -*Ragu R., Assistant Professor, KSG Education Institution, Coimbatore, Tamilnadu.
4. "An Analysis of Psychological Aspects of a Refugee or Migrant as an Effect of Partition in Deepa Mehta's *1947 Earth*"- *Meriya George, Guest Faculty, Department of English, Bharat Mata College, Thrikkakkara.
5. "Developing English Speaking Skills of The Engineering Students Through Drama as Teaching Technique"- *V. Dorothy Catherine, Assistant Professor, Department of English, St. Mary's College (Autonomous), Thoothukudi.
6. "Colonial Gaze: Deconstructing Stereotypical Indian Leads from the Netflix Show *Bridgerton*"- *Ameya Mary Yovakim, Assistant Professor in English, St. Aloysius College, Edathua.
7. "The Empowerment of Women through Sita in Amish Tripathi's *Sita: Warrior of Mithila*" - *Pattam Chakma, Ph. D. Research Scholar, Department of English, Dr. N. G. P. Arts and Science College, Coimbatore, Tamilnadu.
8. "Freaks with Identity: The Female Disabled in Katherine Dunn's *Geek Love*"- *Gayathry Pradeep
9. "Feminine Sensitivity and Psychological Conflict in Anita Desai's *Where Shall We Go This Summer?*"-*Adarsh J.
10. "Reiterating Patriarchy through Stereotyping Family Roles in

Advertisements."- **Harsha Anna Kuriakose**, MA English Language and Literature & MBA in Human Resources, Senior Customer Service Specialist.

11. "Speaking out the Unspoken: Re-Writing the Old Schema of Malayalam Movies in the Twenty First Century"-**Jeelu Elsa Thampi**

12. "The Namesake: Disowning One's Reality"- **Parvathy Varma**

13. "A Study on the Effectiveness of Online Fooding Apps on Registered Restaurants in Alappuzha District with Special Reference to Swiggy and Zomato" - **Sejin Philip George**.

14. "Identity, Trauma and Recovery: *Prison Baby*, A Memoi"-**Roshni Susan Varghese**.

15. "Technology Integrated Practices for English Language Teaching"- **Feba Susan Bejoy**.

16. "Let's Redefine, Reinterpret and Remake the Façade of Disney Personas"-**Adona Alexander**.

17. "Are We Made 'Disabled' By Our Own Society? An Analysis of the Novel *Mahashweta* Through the Lens of Disability Studies" -**Andria Joseph**.

18. "Ecocidal Imagination: A Study on J.G. Ballarad's *The Drought*"-**Betsy Sebastian**.

Editor

Dr. Saran S.
Editor-in-Chief
Edit Academic Publication

Dr. Saran S., is a writer, Poet, Nature Activist, Teacher, and Research Scholar. He completed his Doctoral Research at the Department of English, M. S. University in 2020. Currently, he is working as an Assistant Professor and Head in the Department of English, University Institute of Technology Pathiyoor, University of Kerala. His areas are Comparative Literature, Cultural Studies, Film Studies, Psychoanalytical Studies and Eco Studies. He is the author of several articles published in various national and international journals as well as six academic books on topics of current interest like English Language, Film Studies, Partition Studies and Cultural Studies. He also authored a collection of poems and short stories. He also edited twenty-four international books. He is the chief editor of Edit Academic, an advisory board member and Associate Editor in *The Creative Launcher*, international, open access, peer-reviewed refereed, e-journal in English and also an Editorial Board Member in *Shodhkosh: Journal of Visual and Performing Arts* (UGC-Care Listed Journal).

• • •

Editor

Dona Mathew
Editorial Board Member
Edit Academic Publication

Dona Mathew is an aspiring researcher and writer based on Kerala, India. She holds her M. A. in English Language and Literature and B. Ed. Degree from Mahatma Gandhi University, Kottayam, Kerala. She did her M.Phil. from Bharathiar University, Coimbatore, Tamil Nadu. She also served as a Freelance Content Writer (Elearn College, London) as well as the Editor of various publications. She also has a number of presentations and publications to her credit. Her areas of interest include Literary and Critical Theory, Postcolonial Studies, Gender and Sexuality Studies, Feminism, Medical Humanities, etc. She is currently an English teacher at Marthoma Residential School, Thiruvalla, Kerala

Introduction

BRICOLAGE

"If one calls bricolage the necessity of borrowing one's concepts from the text of a heritage
which is more or less coherent or ruined, it must be said that every discourse is bricoleur."

-Jacques Derrida, *Structure, Sign, and Play*

Greetings dear readers! We are extremely delighted and proud to introduce the new book *BRICOLAGE*. It is a collection of a number of research papers by academic aspirants. It helped them to discuss, present and publish valuable papers on multidisciplinary areas and internationalise their research works. This book is committed to bring together academicians, research scholars and students who work professionally to upgrade the status of academic realm and society by their ideas and aims to promote interdisciplinary studies. The French anthropologist Claude Levi-Strauss, in his book *The Savage Mind* (1966), used the word bricolage for the first time. On the practical level, bricolage takes objects that have been used before and reorganizes them within a new perspective.

Bricolage is the skill of using whatever is at hand and recombining them to create something new. The bricoleur (a person who does bricolage) is the "savage mind" who works with his/ her hands in devious ways, puts pre-existing things together in new ways, and makes do with whatever is at hand. The materials of a bricoleur are already been used and can be used again. Every finite discourse is bound by a certain bricolage. Bricolage understands meaning not as something eternal and immutable, but as something provisional, something shifting. The system of language, of which every text is made, too has no discernible center.

The postmodern art practices and architecture, intertextuality in Literature, subcultures and new cultural identities, social and psychological bricolage, mythical thought in Philosophy multiperspectival research and multimethodological inquiry in Education, "bricoleur style" of programming/coding, bricolage-like styles in fashion industry, certain religious behaviours in modern societies, etc. are few examples. The idea of bricolage produces a new way to talk and think about systems and structures, practices radical experimentation, without falling into the trap of trying to build a new stable system out of the ruins of a deconstructed one. It provides a way to think without establishing a new center, a privileged reference, an origin, a truth. It also inspires creativity, making possible new ways of putting things together.

Bricolage is not simply a metaphor, but a universal concept, indeed an essence of modern scientific and technological development. This book is a practice of bricolage by a number of bricoleurs, who refused to accept the limitations of their environment and the notion of a single 'truth', and believed in the process of the 'decentralisation' of power. May each word and idea in this book become the resources for the upcoming bricoleurs. Research should be instrumental in generating a major interface with the academic world. It must provide a new theoretical framework that enable reassessment and refinement of current practices. This may result in some major discoveries and an extension of the acquired knowledge. It empowers the faculty, students and teachers for an in-depth approach in research. It even enhances the consultancy capabilities of the researcher. In short, the main objective of this book is to provide a common platform for educational reformation through research.

The book covers research papers on a number of topics and research areas such as Feminism, women empowerment and gender, Cartoon and Graphic Studies, Colonial stereotype, Critical Race Studies, Disability studies, Ecocriticism, Theatre and English language instruction, Cross- culturalism, Technology and English language teaching, Cultural Studies, Media, art and cyber space, Partition studies, Identity and Diasporic Literature, War Literature, Trauma Studies, E-Commerce, etc. We are sure that this selfless effort of pooling in research papers will enlighten the readers. We also express a humble note of gratitude to all the contributors. We are indeed grateful to all who have been with us since the inception of the book.

Wishing every reader a fruitful reading!

ELEMENTS OF MODERNISM AND POST-MODERNISM IN THE SELECTED NOVELS OF AMIT CHAUDHURI

Dr. Roselin Linitta George M. A., M. Phil., Ph. D.
Assistant Professor in English
Sanpada College of Commerce and Technology
Navi Mumbai, Maharashtra

ABSTRACT

Amit Chaudhuri is a modern writer whose writings showcase modern, post-modern, and regional elements. Calcutta is the city that becomes the background of his works. With his modern techniques, he converts the mundane and microelements to macroelements, thus providing universal appeal to the story, characters, and background of his novels. This paper is an attempt to seek and discuss modern and post-modern elements in the selected novels of Amit Chaudhuri. Amit Chaudhuri is a novelist, a critic, and an essayist. He has written seven novels so far, anon fictional book, an anthology, an acritical book, and two-story books. His novels include *A Strange and Sublime Address* (1991), *Afternoon Raag* (1993), *Freedom Song* (1998), *A New World* (2000), *The Immortals* (2009), *Odysseus Abroad* (2014), and *Friend of My Youth* (2017).

Elements of Modernism and Post-Modernism in the Selected Novels of Amit Chaudhuri

• • •

Indian society is a society that gladly soaks up all cultures and elements and amalgamates tradition and modernity. Modernism in Indian society is a result of continuously changing traditions and updated values. In a way traditions transformed into their modern forms thus creating a happy amalgamation of tradition and modernity. Modernization is an ongoing elastic process that incorporates culture well.

Amit Chaudhuri, in his critical book, 'Clearing a Space' clears that his intention "-is to propose an alternative story of modernity and modernism; to distinguish it from both European modernism and the narrative of post-coloniality"(53). Modernism became a genre of fiction writing in the 1910s and 1960s. The effects of world war, new technology, industrialization, capitalism and globalization brought new trends in the literature as well. The term 'Modern' denotes something new that is discovered, achieved, or done in the contemporary period and 'Modernism' refers to the use of modernist elements thus experimenting with the set literary form. The inner self and inner consciousness were focused upon by the writers in their works. Alienation, nostalgia, depressive tendencies and loneliness became the watchwords of modernism and post-modernism. New techniques like irony, satire, comparisons, Magic Realism, Intersexuality, Pastiche, Metafiction, Fragmentation, different Perspectives and stream of consciousness were employed. The writers like T.S. Eliot. Sylvia Plath, William Faulkner, William Butler Yeats, Ezra Pound, Ernest Hemmingway, Virginia Woolf and D. H. Lawrence are the writers of the modern era.

Post-modernism is a departure from modernism in the wake of the second world war. It redefines the modern in a new sense. New forms were experimented upon and new techniques were relied upon freely in post-modernism. Some key figures like Samuel Beckett, Jorge Luis Borges and Gabriel Garcia Marquez are the main supporters of post-modern times.

Many Indian English writers of the 20th century were connected to foreign culture by being brought up in a foreign country or by going abroad for higher education. Eventuallyfew of them get settled abroad. They employ Indian themes to write in the English language and style. Orthodox thoughts and traditional values were questioned by these writers in their works. The key elements of Post Modern Indian English fiction are the broadening of thematic range, the cultural encounters between east and west, love, sex, marriage and its future, lack faith in religion and decline of moral standards and behavior, feminism, realism, nationalism and use of myths and stream of consciousness techniques, etc. The names of a few such writers of 20th century include Amitav Ghosh, V. S. Naipul, Chitra Banerjee Divakaruni, Gita Mehta, Anita Desai, Kiran Desai, Bharti Mukherjee, Rohinton Mistry, Amit Chaudhuri, Jhumpa Lahiri, Namita Gokhale, Siddharth Dhawan, Vikram Chandra, etc.

In the chapter Notes on the Novel after Globalization, in the critical work of the novelist himself, Clearing a Space he expresses his views on Modernity in the modern sense. Modernity is the last phase of humanism and is caught between its two resonances: between progress and the perfectibility of the human on the one hand, and nostalgia and loss on the other. Modernism aestheticizes this in a new and influential way: the avant-garde, for instance, is enmeshed in the vocabulary of development, in the idea of the 'breakthrough', of being at the forefront, at the vanguard – and, at the same time, it ironizes development, for its experiments rehabilitate broken, unfinished forms, at odds with the social completeness that the world around the artistic fraternity strives for (207).

Amit Chaudhuri has expressed modernism and post-modernism in his novels through characters, realism, situations in narration, and the use of modern devices and techniques. In the novel 'A Strange and Sublime Address, the effects of industrialization, globalization and modernization are clearly visible in the city and over the lives of people.

The first novel, A Strange and Sublime Address presents the story of Calcutta through the eyes of the protagonist Sandeep. The story is of a joint family in Calcutta. Sandeep visits his Chotomama's house along with his parents and loves every bit of the time, he spends in the city. The novel tells the story of the city of Calcutta and the changing trends in the wake of modernization. The adults and their problems of survival in the city, in the face of financial burdens, add the element of realism to the novel. The environmental consciousness of Sandeep is also a modernistic element. Social realism portrays the hardships and struggles of the middle class, the troubles of breadwinners and the financial burden become a prominent factor of the novel. The maternal uncle of Sandeep, Chhotamama has invested all his savings into a business. His car troubled him a lot but he could not afford a new one and at last, started going to the office by bus. His struggles resonate with the struggles of a modern man.

Feminism, another element of modernism is also present in a slightly different way in the novel. Bengali society is a woman–dominated society where female members are more dominant than male folks. The characters of Mamima and Sandeep's mother, make the novel splashed with colours of liveliness. The confidence of these two female characters running the household is praiseworthy. The novel also uses various literary devices like use of simile, metaphor, irony and images. The technique of defamiliarization is also used in describing the prayer routine of Mamima.

The second novel by Amit Chaudhuri is set in Oxford where the narrator stays for further studies and feels depressed and nostalgic in the empty civilization devoid of true sensibilities. He could not adjust to the place, faces an identity crisis and misses his mother and his home constantly. The narrator mentions the place, "Oxford is a place where every year "...new students come and old ones disappear;" (5). The students stay here for studies and leave after exams making "the town nearly empty" (5). They leave behind the "old way of life" (6) and study in a city that is "dreamlike" (6). The narrator's comment of western civilization as an "empty bastion of civilization and citizenry" (6). Multiculturalism or imagining or thinking and the presence and adoption of various cultures in one place is a frequently used tool of the writer in 'Afternoon Raag'.

The third novel 'Freedom Song' is set in the city of Bombay which is overburdened by economic upheavals and rising communalism in the wake of the Babri Masjid-related riots. The title itself is ironic pointing out the lost freedom. This novel describes a transitional phase between departing tradition and commencing modernity. The novel is written in a realistic manner with a narrative that moves backward and forward in time.

In the novel "A New World", the protagonist Jayojit returns back to India from America along with his son Bonny, in search of his identity, after a painful divorce from his wife Amala. He is welcomed by his parents who are living their married life with peacefulness and a set routine. Jayojit though comes for solace, seems to be hanging between both worlds traditional ad modern, throughout the novel and is not ready to compromise. He feels detachment, disorientation, rootlessness and dilemma, all products of modern rotten society.The novel uses flashback and stream-of-consciousness techniques like spatialization and temporalization of space, reflexivity, ambiguity and fragmented narrative.

Another novel of Amit Chaudhuri, 'Odysseus Abroad', employs the stream of consciousness technique where the protagonist Ananda is a modern man who is fond of modern writers of English and American literature, like Philip Larkin, D.H.Lawrence etcetera; thus adding an autobiographical touch to the novel. The novel describes a day in the life of Ananda, spent along with his uncle Radhesh where a small journey is made from Ananda's place to Radhesh's place and both explore the city physically and revolving in their pasts mentally. Ananda is interested in many things including the politics of the country. He is a modern man with mixed views. When he sees the concert at Wembley stadium on the TV, he is reminded of the famine-stricken country of Ethiopia. He felt as if he is isolated from the whole world and London itself. He feels aloof to the point that he even stopped participating in many things at college. He feels that being an Indian he is insulted by being ruled by the country where he is currently residing. England may be in confusion about changing political scenario still Ananda cannot forget the pain of subjugation.

Multiculturalism or the depiction of multiracial culture becomes a tool in the hands of post-modern novelists, The reference to the

Chinese, their discomfort with the city, and Ananda's awkward approach pave a way for the creation of a new culture where all can adjust well and feel at home. It is a quest to find oneself in the changing world. Amit Chaudhuri creates a mythical cocktail like a true connoisseur. Ulysses and Joyce resonate in the journey of Ananad to Radhesh in the wake of the journey of Telemachus.

Another and to date, the last novel of Amit chaudhuri is Friend Of My Youth which presents a fine interplay of memory and reality and tradition and modernity. The narrator thinks about his connections with Bombay and at the same time shifts his gaze to his England days and after a short sojourn, comes back to his reality. There is a connectivity between the last line of each part and the beginning line of another past which is adopted by the novelist. One can also find a sudden transition from past to present, past to future, and vice-versa.

The attack in Mumbai and its terror of aftermath form the background of the novel. The usually bright city, bright with sounds becomes silent with an attack. "With the armed men having alighted at two different spots from dinghies, the sea hems in the city. It's ineluctable. The city isn't sure what to do with it"(Chaudhuri "Friend" 49). And at Taj, he could sense the loss, "Those men made for this wing, of course, and the cat and mouse game lasted four days. People fleeing, hiding, dying, changing location at strange hours, led by staff" (45-46). In his critical work, Amit Chaudhuri finely points out the changing trends of literature calling this change "a new mythology of travel, displacement, movement, and settlement with, paradoxically, its new anxious awareness of the 'other', the foreign and the native" (12).

Thus the novels of Amit Chaudhuri finely showcase modern and postmodern elements, resulting in an amalgamation of both, turning them into a sought-after and to-be-followed style for the new generation of writers who are constantly pacing between both worlds, traditional and modern, like the novelist himself.

Works Cited

Chaudhuri, Amit. *Afternoon Raag*. India: Penguin Books,2012.

--- A *New World*. India: Penguin Books, 2012.

---*A Strange and Sublime Address*. India: Penguin Books, 2012.

---*Clearing a Space: Reflections on India, literature, and culture.* India: Penguin Books, 2012.

---*Freedom song,* India: Penguin Books, 2012.

---*Friend of My Youth*. India: Penguin Books, 2017.

---*Odysseus Abroad*. India, Penguin Books, 2014.

---*The Immortals*. India: Penguin Books, 2012.

THE PORTRAYAL OF BICULTURAL DAUGHTERS AND IMMIGRANT MOTHERS IN AMY TAN'S TWO KINDS

Dr. B. Muthulakshmi M. A., Ph. D.
Assistant Professor, Department of English
Manonmaniam Sundaranar University
Abishekapatti, Tirunelveli -12.

ABSTRACT

This paper outlines the specific ways in which the bicultural daughters depicted in Amy Tan's *Two Kinds* struggle with identifying themselves with their mothers' cultures and the dominating American culture in which they grow – up. It correlates the relationships between immigrant mothers and their bicultural daughters and provides examples of this bond as viewed in this short – story. This study brings out the prominence of current criticism, the struggles portrayed in the story that a bicultural daughter deals with while attempting to revive her mother's culture while being forced to adapt to the dominant culture.

Keywords: Cross – Culturalism, American Culture, Bicultural Daughters and Immigrant Mothers.

**The portrayal of Bicultural Daughters and Immigrant
Mothers in Amy Tan's *Two Kinds***

• • •

Amy Tan is one of the most original and dynamic Asian – American writers of American Literature. She has strongly affiliated herself with two driving forces in the literary world of the late twentieth century: cross-culturalism and feminism. This positive union of themes and style does not surface from a planned attempt to maneuver the fiction world but from Amy Tan's internal struggles with self, society, their mother, and the past. Amy Tan herself parallels the first – generation Chinese – American characters who people her top–selling inter–generational works, *The Joy Luck Club* (1989), *The Kitchen God's Wife* (1991), and *The Hundred Secret Senses* (1995). Influenced by the stories of memorable women throughout her mother's life, Amy Tan has in these works honored a sisterhood whose power and vigor are as inspirational to her writing as her typical cultural upbringing.

It is significant to read and understand mixed-race stories because they give us a chance for us to open our eyes, to acquire new perspectives, and thus revive ourselves. Taking his concept a step further, the prominence of analyzing mixed and bi-cultural stories to acquire new perspectives on the ever-changing world is perceived in the very makeup of contemporary America – a nation where more and more people are identifying as ethnically and culturally fused. By examining literature that has been penned by and about bi-cultural people, specifically bicultural women, the challenges encountered by this marginalized group will extend what it means to be an American woman with multiple identities.

The prevailing ideas of race in America require, multicultural and bicultural, authors to choose one identity, thus erasing others that they might believe. This is the reason why daughters in mixed race and cultural literature manage to have tough relationships with their mothers. They regard themselves to be "American" and belonging to their mother's culture, but the prevalent culture in America – and sometimes even the immigrant mother – tells bicultural daughters to choose only one, leaving no space for hybridization. And multicultural and bicultural authors are possibly to create characters who struggle with their identity because that is what happens to them. If the author's writing is set in that society, the characters will also have such struggles.

"Two Kinds" is a short – story in Amy Tan's hugely successful maiden novel, *The Joy Luck Club*. She intended the novel to be read as a loose collection of interconnected stories, but it is mostly referred to as a novel. Most of the short – stories come out in periodicals which purchased the serial rights to the book prior to its publication. It is initially published in Atlantic Monthly in February 1989, one month before the book is released. In "Two Kinds" Jing–Mei learns something new from her mother's tales as well. In this short story, one sees that compliance with the ethnic culture often comes when the daughter has grown up and is recollecting the tales that her mother used to recount "America was where all my mother's hopes lay. She had come to San Francisco in 1949 after losing everything in China: her mother and father, her family, her first husband, and two daughters, twin baby girls. But she never looked back with regret. Things could get better in so many ways" (258).

In "Two Kinds", Jing – Mei's mother only narrates one story – the story of her twin sisters who passed away in China. Jing–Mei's mother attempts to implant her Chinese moral beliefs of how an ideal woman must behave in her American daughter by storytelling – a correlation to the homeland's concept of identity. In "Placing Identity in Cross-Cultural Perspective," Anne E. Brown and Marjanne E. Gooze write that "no single or fixed definition of identity can be universally applied" (xiii). This present paper also discusses the relationship with another Chinese – American family portrayed through "Two Kinds." Amy Tan was born in America to immigrant Chinese parents. Yet, she is unambiguous that her first-person short – story "Two Kinds" is fictional. Even though it can stand alone as a short – story since it also has been published separately in the Atlantic Monthly – "Two Kinds" is a slice of the novel, *The Joy Luck Club*.

A story becomes universal when the reader is brought into the story by the storyteller who is also the protagonist. And when the narrator is disclosing her emotions and experiences growing up, all readers can connect better or will want to connect to such instances. The narrator in "Two Kinds" has grown up and is writing retrospectively of her childhood days in a universal manner. "Two Kinds" happens totally in America. The central character and narrator Jing – Mei grows up in San Francisco in the 1950s. Due to her nightmarish experiences back home in China, just as long as she attains perfection.

It is due to these pressures from so-called phenomenal prodigies that Jing-Mei grows to neglect her mother, in spite of her mother's purpose. After being questioned on things such as the state capitals of America, capital cities in Europe, magic – tricks, and other memorabilia, Jing-Mei grows bored of her mother's strategies. More so, she feels embarrassed because she cannot quite reach her mother's ethics.

Jing-Mei feels that her accomplishment is bonded to her appearance. Jing-Mei has learned that a prosperous Chinese woman in America accomplishes greatness with both her proficiency and her gorgeous look. But despite Jing–Mei's mother wishing for her to become a prodigy of talents and looks, an ethnic she seems to have assimilated the American society, Jing-Mei still perceives an unpleasantness about herself when she cannot reach her mother's ethics. And it is through this anguish of not feeling good enough that Jing-Mei realizes that she does not want to become the child her mother wants her to be. It is Jing–Mei's mother's Chinese spirit that leads Jing–Mei into the American condition. By revolting against her mother – in spite of having internalized American ethics for her daughter's welfare – the girl is renouncing her mother's dreams and stating an identity devoid of perfection.

Part of the plan to remain unaffected by her mother includes Jing–Mei not taking her daily piano classes sincerely. Indeed, Jing-Mei's tutor is partly deaf and partly blind, making it effortless for Jing-Mei to "be lazy and get away with mistakes, lots of mistakes" (263). To such an extent that Jing-Mei extremely embarrasses her parents at a local talent show because she is unrehearsed. After playing her terrible recital of the piece "Pleading Child" – whose title itself connotes the inadequacy of a baby – Jing–Mei feels "the shame of [her] mother and father as they sat stiffly though the rest of the show" (265).

It is not until this feud between the two that one can see the mother's loss while fleeing China years before as being a supporting factor to the bond between Chinese – American Jing-Mei and her immigrant mother. Moreover, all of the habits and rituals that Jing–Mei's mother forced her to endure paid off in the end because she now plays the piano well enough. After all these years, it is not until Jing–Mei plays both pieces that she realizes just how intensely she remains bonded with her mother. Because, unlike her mother, Jing-Mei "did not believe I could be anything I wanted to be" (267) – an American belief that her mother has adopted for her daughter. Because Jing-Mei is both Chinese and American, growing up she thought that her hybridity meant that she could not become great. And so, rather than living up to her nightmares of failure, she rather failed to live up to her mother's dreams of success. It is not until going back to her mother's residence as an adult that Jing-Mei realizes that it is possible to be both pleading and content. Amy Tan overstates the clash that drives a "balanced blend," admitting the Chinese and the American attitudes toward herself coexist. "Two Kinds" perfectly portrays the struggles that an immigrant mother and her bicultural daughter endure, and bring awareness to this specific mother-daughter combination in America.

WORKS CITED

Brown, Anne E and Marjanne E Gooze. "Placing Identity in Cross-Cultural Perspective."
International Women's Writing: New Landscapes of Identity. Greenwood Press, 1995, pp. xiii-xxv.

Foster, Marie Booth. "Voice, Mind, Self: Mother – Daughter Relationships in Amy Tan's *The*
Joy Luck Club and *The Kitchen God's Wife* and *Women of Color.* U of Texas Press, 1996, pp. 208 – 27.

Tan, Amy. "Two Kinds." *Atlantic Monthly*, vol. 263, no. 2, 1989, pp. 53 – 57.

BIO – NOTE

Dr. B. Muthulakshmi, native of Tirunelveli, Tamilnadu, holds a Doctorate in English from Manonmaniam Sundaranar University, Tirunelveli. Her research interest includes Canadian Literature and Indian Literature. She has completed her Under-Graduation and

Post-Graduation in English from V.O.C. College, Tuticorin. She has presented many papers in both National and International Conferences and attended many workshops related to Literature.

CHAPTER III

THE PSYCHOLOGY OF MARTYRDOM IN DANIELLE STEEL'S FLYING ANGELS

Ragu R. M. A., B. Ed., M. Phil.
Assistant Professor, KSG Education Institution
Coimbatore, Tamilnadu

ABSTRACT

The paper tries to have an analysis of the six fighter nurses, their lives, contributions and sacrifices during World War II, as depicted in the book *Flying Angels* by Danielle Steel. The book takes us back to the late 1930s and early 1940s as brave women nurses enlist. The focus is on their self-sacrifice, martyrdom, women empowerment, and other social differences such as racism of the time. Martyrdom is defined as the psychological readiness to suffer and sacrifice one's life for a cause. The nurses have sacrificed their lives and some even became martyrs for the freedom of their country. They risked their lives the same as any male soldiers. The "Flying Angels" are true heroes.

Keywords: Flying angels, fighting nurses, self-sacrifice, martyrdom, psychology, women empowerment, and social differences.

The Psychology of Martyrdom in Danielle Steel's Flying Angels

• • •

The setting of the novel was World War II when Pearl Harbour was attacked by Japan. It brings together six remarkable young American and English nurses who face the challenges of war. The six women- Audrey, Lizzie, Alex, Louise, Pru, and Emma- become fast friends as they work tirelessly for the war effort and risk their lives every day to bring the wounded back to hospitals in England.

Their bravery and courage are remarkable as they joined the Medical Air Evacuation Transport Squadron to fly into enemy territory almost daily to rescue wounded soldiers from the battlefield.

When it comes to war stories, the plot would be narrated about the soldiers. However, here we can see the self-sacrifice of women in each family who sacrificed their life and enlisted their names in the army as fighter nurses. Six flying angels in the novel have enlisted as army flight nurses and saved many lives. They flew into enemy territory almost daily to rescue wounded soldiers from the battlefield. Among them, two nurses from a well posh family are Alexandra and Prudence who have left their comfortable life and lived their adventures in the battle.

Audrey and her friend Lizzie were fresh out of the nursing school. Audrey had already lost her brother a Navy man in the beginning of the war. Alex wanted to make a difference in the world through her life. Louise was a black woman, a bright mind from the south who was raised by parents in the medical field but faces segregation and racism every day. Prudence was a selfless woman, Emma, a confident, grit woman.

There are so many instances in the book that shows the dedication, bravery as well as the affection among the fighter nurses. When Louise returned to her base and five days later Paris was liberated from German also. The news was spread that five hundred resistance fighters were killed in the battle. Only nine of them were saved by the team of Louise. War was at the severe end where Prudence and her team went to pick up men in Argonne Forest the field near the American 12th Evacuation hospital. Ed did not accompany her as he was with Lizzie so, when Prudence was on her mission the pilots and with co-pilot also with two crops men in C-47, was shot down by the two fighter planes of German headed towards them, though Reggie tried a lot she could not save that day. Among the dead soldier's names, Prudence was one of the best fighter nurses that the team faced a great loss.

Emma could not take it that her dearest friend is been killed and when she is packing all of Prudence's things, she got a personal dairy and she went on reading what Prudence has written about her family and her brothers and of every memory she spent with her family in the house and especially she has also written too many pages about Emma and her funny talks with her, their experience when they lost in the forest. Emma wanted to send this diary to her parents by herself so she did not think about anything else and got ready to visit Prudence's house. She took a train to Yorkshire that too the environment was very bad during wartime, had unreliable rain schedules and bombing raids. She did not think about anything but she is from East End and where she is going to is a posh family where she could be welcomed or thrown away with insult.

Finally, she is at the door and Max opened the door and looked surprised to see Emma, and Prudence's mother welcomed Emma with warm hug and they were nice to her and asked her to stay with them as it was Christmas Eve. Emma gave the diary to Prudence's mother and Emma had a nice time with Max, both have talked only about Prudence. Max is always proud of her sister and she is the best flying Angels. The next day Emma left the house with Prudence's diary because Prudence's mother gave it back to Emma as she decided it would be precious when it was with Emma and both Max and Emma were back at the base to their work.

Another heart-breaking news was ready for the nurses as another talented flight nurse Audrey and her team was shot down by the fighter pilots. Lizzie met another great loss of her dearest friend, though Audrey has nothing to lose as she dedicated all her life to nursing others. Lizzie was at her grief as she does not know how many will be dead in this war. Audrey had left her will in her room and Lizzie read it fully. Audrey did not have any family to look after her house so she transferred her authority on the house to Lizzie's name and it was the gift of Christmas Eve to Lizzie. When Lizzie had plans with Ed to study and stay together this would financially help Lizzie in her life.

Among the six flying angels, the two greatest fighters were dead when the war comes to an end. Their loss cannot be replaced. The novel comes to an end with the award-giving ceremony to the fighter nurses. Medical Air Evacuation Transport Squadron wore their uniform dresses for this ceremony. Everyone was given a medal for their extreme services and especially six women were named posthumously for services to the country and their bravery in combat. They were Prudence, Audrey, Emma, Louise, Alexandra, and Lizzie. As Gonzague promised he was in that ceremony with Louise and he is soon going to be the Legion of Honour.

After the ceremony, Lizzie was in her room the next day and an air force commander was waiting to see her and she started crying as she knows he is not there to bring her good news, as in the last great battle of the war in the Pacific, her brother Henry had been killed in the battle of Okinawa. Lizzie had lost two of her brothers and her best friend Audrey and she has nothing to lose in her life. In the beginning, when she wanted to go to medical school and become a doctor or get a job in the New York, her parents thought that a woman does not need to achieve as a doctor and they gave all their opportunities to the men in the family. But now there is a no men in their family to survive, the only member who survived is Lizzie sustained all of the battles and saved dozens of lives, also underwent both physical and mental fitness now, she received an award as 'the best fighter nurse'.

After five days of ceremony, it was time to leave the base and there was a huge crowd of nurses from the Air Evacuation Squadron saying goodbye and leaving for home but they had become a family though they have faced losses in the battle. They shared a pure bond and be the strength of unstable patients and sustained many of soldiers' life.

Alexandra, Lizzie, and Louise climbed the stairs to the transport plane on the tarmac and they waved their hands to all their other friends and everyone was ready to leave. They were together at the tough times, love and affection for each other were strong and has no difference in their mind at the end of the war.

In the novel *Flying Angels* by, we could see the self-sacrifice of every woman in the family who has dedicated their life to them and for the country. Family members were proud of their sons who had died in war as well as there are fighter nurses who were dead in the battle like Prudence and Audrey. They lived a saluting life and their parents were equally proud of their daughters who have participated in the war.

In common, the term "martyrdom" describes the personality of a person who blames the people and the society around for their failures and depression then goes to the extreme of persecuting themselves to avoid their responsibilities. But in psychological concept of martyrdom a person sacrifices everything they have and may be their situations forces them to sacrifice their life but they do it wholeheartedly with devotion for the sake of their family members and for the country. Hence, we can find the devotional sacrifices with the soldiers fighting in the war. In the book *Flying Angels*, the concept of 'psychological martyrdom' of self- sacrifice is totally there. That is the power of human to admit all of wordily affairs as one side and the rather other part of courage to face death any time and to give away the life for the country and for the people.

Six protagonists in the book Audrey, Lizzie, Louise, Alexandra, Prudence and Emma have different lives but have the common perception of freedom. That is independence to live, like, love and die. They all had depressions and more of dominations from the society and family but they did not blame them instead they chose to either live as warrior or die as soldiers but not to return to the snobbish environment.

Audrey is the main element of self-sacrifice who lived only for her family and then for the country and faced brave death. Lizzie who is Audrey's friend resembles the modern thoughts of equality for men and women and stood against her family and enlisted in the army. Emma and Louise are the symbols to show the social differences that prevail in the society in the name of a language, living standards, and racial discrimination. Emma and Louise symbolize the differences that prevail in the society based on the upper class and lower-class society, and still there are snobbish differences between East End accents and British and American accents. Among those things, racial discrimination dominates the people and their thoughts of differences.

Even in the twenty- first century, many women are under the domination of family circumstances and their rules. Audrey sacrificed her entire life from adulthood to the end without any ecstasy in life. She enlisted her name in the army as she could sacrifice her life for a reason of service to the country. When Lizzie had the same situation of thinking about the brave death of Captain Will and she too equals a tough fighter nurse who has saved as many lives as she could.

Prudence and Alexandra were from a high society family and they sacrificed their comfortable life to have some adventures and new experiences in life. When other members of the family were dressed in long gowns and ornaments to attend the ball as if nothing had happened in the world, both Prudence and Alexandra wore a sack green, solid shirt and trousers nothing less to a man. These feminist fighter nurses depict the contribution of women in the war and their empowerment.

Though the war has given a lot of pain and deaths, more dark dreams behind all, it has given a chance to forget all the differences and united them to fight together. When the family members showed their choice of life to the women in their family, they fought for their rights and in the end, they proved that women were equal and made their families proud of their work and sacrifices in the war. Ultimately, the flying angels had shown what women empowerment truly was. Even knowing they will not achieve any rank and will receive little pay for their efforts, the "Flying Angels" gave their all in the fight for freedom. They serve as bravely and tirelessly as the men they rescue on the front lines, in daring airlifts, and are eternally bound by their loyalty to one another. They are inspiring symbols of bravery and valour.

In a nutshell, *Flying Angels* depicts the sacrifices made by a woman inside the family or on her day-to-day work. People have more of stress and depression in their life but on counting its level, it is higher for a woman to stand up with all of dominations put on her and restrictions made on her choices to live a life. What she wants to do in her life, better she will choose death as a greater one than facing those challenges that are becoming harder in today's scenario. But her determination never changes to bring a revolution in the society.

WORKS CITED

Daniel Fernande Schuelein-Steel. Flying Angels: Delacorte Press an imprint of Random House a division of Penguin Random House LLC, New York, 23rd of November 2021.

Sophia Moskalenko, Clark McCauley. The Marvel of Martyrdom: Oxford University Press. 2019.

BIO - NOTE

Ragu Rajendran is currently working as Assistant Professor of English at Coimbatore. He also serves as the coordinator of the Youth Red Cross Club, Photography and Short Film Club. He specialises in storytelling and creative writing. He is skilful in both academics and in competitive fields. An avid reader, he enjoys playing with words. He loves coffee, books and movies. He is inspired daily by his parents, students and professors.

CHAPTER IV

AN ANALYSIS OF PSYCHOLOGICAL ASPECTS OF A REFUGEE OR MIGRANT AS AN EFFECT OF PARTITION IN DEEPA MEHTA'S 1947 EARTH

Meriya George M. A., B. Ed.
  Guest Faculty, Department of English,
  Bharat Mata College, Thrikkakkara.

ABSTRACT

Historical and historiographical works about partition have their own values and place. Literature has a vital role to play in preserving events in collective memory and interpreting the implications for posterity. The partition and the bloody riots have inspired many writers in India and Pakistan to create literary as well as cinematic depictions of the events. Some may concentrate on the riots and massacres of the refugees as such during the migration. Others depict the aftermath of the partition. The trauma left by Partition remains a significant concern of Indian literature after independence. Partition led to widespread massacres, rape, terror, rioting, hostility, distrust, religious intolerance, and enmity. One of the most famous cinematic depictions of the partition events in India was Deepa Mehta's *1947 Earth*, released in 1998, which was an adaptation of Bapsi Sidhwa's Ice Candy Man. This paper tries to say that partition is not just a physical phenomenon, but the idea of partition and dividing the nation or minds into two geographical lands happen first. Thus, partition becomes a psychological phenomenon too.

Key Terms: Partition, trauma, and migration.

An Analysis of Psychological Aspects of a Refugee or Migrant as an Effect of Partition in Deepa Mehta's *1947 Earth*

• • •

Partition is commonly understood as dividing a state into two or more entities, where at least one successor states assume continuity with the pre-divided whole. The most famous partitions in history happened after the end of colonialism. Partitions of Ireland, India, Palestine, etc. are examples. The partition is usually followed by the migration of peoples as refugees to another land, maybe from the existing motherland to the newly formed dominion. India's case also was not different. Over one million people were killed during India's division. Seven million Muslims and five million Hindus and Sikhs were uprooted in the largest and most terrible exchange of population known to history.

Historical and historiographical works about partition have their own values and place. Literature has a vital role to play in preserving events in collective memory and interpreting the implications for posterity. The partition and the bloody riots have inspired many writers in India and Pakistan to create literary as well as cinematic depictions of the events. Some may concentrate on the riots and massacres of the refugees as such during the migration. Others depict the aftermath of the partition.

The trauma left by Partition remains a significant concern of Indian literature after independence. Partition led to widespread massacres, rape, terror, rioting, hostility, distrust, religious intolerance, and enmity. Creative minds adopted these themes and illustrated them in the form of poetry, fiction, prose, and cinema. Another common theme was the restoration of humanism and propagation of communal harmony after the partition. Communal narrow-mindedness and religious fanaticism were the prime reasons behind the riots following the partition. The real sorrow of the partition was that it brought an abrupt end to a long history of communal coexistence. This does not mean that they had a very good relationship prior to the partition. But it is to be remembered that Hindus never ceased paying homage to *dargahs*, Muslims continued to participate in Hindu festivals. Traders of both communities carried on with their usual exchange of goods and services. This coexistence came to a sudden halt and it was replaced by intolerance, rage, and hatred. Each religion saw another as a fanatic group that is liable for the destruction of the peace in the country. They started finding faults with the other ones. The partition brought irreparable damage to the country.

Gita Vishwanatha and Salma Malik quote Mushirul Hasan regarding two parallel events making a history of the Indian subcontinent.

"No other country in the twentieth century has seen two such contrary movements taking place at the same time. If one was popular nationalist movement, the other was the counter movement of the partition, marked by violence, cruelty, bloodshed, displacement and massacres." (2009:61)

Thus, we can say that the year 1947 was considered to be a year of joy and tragedy. Of joy, because India got independence from the British Empire. Of tragedy, because the dream of a united India was shattered, forever.

One of the most famous cinematic depictions of the partition events in India was Deepa Mehta's *1947 Earth*, released in 1998, which was an adaptation of Bapsi Sidhwa's Ice Candy Man. The book *Ice Candy Man* penned by Sidhwa, a Pakistani writer, was published in the year 1988 and was republished in 1991 and titled *Cracking India*. The novel deals with the aftermath of the partition of India. The book narrates the "bloody" partition of India through the eyes of Lenny, an eight-year-old Parsee girl. The plot is set in Lahore, one of the most affected places during the Indo-Pak Partition.

Deepa Mehta, the Indo-Canadian filmmaker is famous for her Element Trilogy- *Fire* (1996), *Earth* (1998), and *Water* (2005). Mehta's *Fire* turns out to be one of the first Indian movies which deal with homosexuality. Water was quite a controversial movie that depicts the life of widows. The movie was banned in India due to the commotion that followed its making of the movie. Water opened the 2005 Toronto International Film Festival and was nominated for an Academy Award for Best Foreign Language Film in 2006.

Earth comes second in the Element Trilogy, following *Fire*. The movie depicts the riots, massacres, and abuses following the partition in the place called Lahore. The story is narrated by an eight-year-old Parsee girl Lenny, who is a crippled one through the voice of her adult self. Even though the main theme is partition and its aftermath, there are parallel stories like the relationship between Lenny and her Ayah, Shanta, a Hindu lady, and the love story of Hassan and Shanta and the admirers of Shanta. The role of little Lenny is played by Maia Sethna, Nandita Das a Shanta, Aamir Khan as Dil Navas, and Rahul Khanna as Hassan. The narrator of the movie is the adult self of Lenny, voiced by Shabana Azmi. 1947 Earth received the Best Film Award at National Film Festival and Rahul Khanna received the Film Fare Best male debut Award. This film was also India's official entry for the 72nd Academy Award for Best Foreign Film. The movie was the first official Oscar-nominated movie from India.

The movie opens with the scene where the title comes in dark letters against a blood-red background. The first scene after the title is where we hear the narration of grown-up Lenny while we see the eight-year-old Lenny coloring the map of India. Lenny, soon after completing the picture rises and then intentionally breaks a glass plate. She asks her mother how English can break the nation into many parts. This opening scene itself has relevance. The whole movie then depicts the bloodshed following the "breaking up of the nation". In the whole film, there is only a very few scenes where we cannot see Lenny. The whole events are her report. Lenny's crippled existence and her nightmarish consciousness represent the state of the nation and the communal apocalyptic condition in contemporary India.

Hassan, the masseur, and Dil Navas, the ice candy man, are in love with Shanta, the maid of Lenny. They meet at the park and have a good time with each other. There are also a few men who have a crush on Shanta. They were good friends but the spark of partition and Hindu-Muslim riots burned the friendship and care that existed between them. Each of them started to uphold one's own religion. Even then, the feelings they had for Shanta kept them together.

"Park has changed. Hindus, Muslims, and Sikhs are keeping to themselves. Only the group around you remains the same. We all hover around you like moths around a lamp." (Film)

From the beginning of the movie, we see the character of Dil Navas as a bit strange. He is a Muslim, who earns his living from different works. Sometimes he sells ice candy, because of which Lenny calls him *Ice Candy wala*. Sometimes he becomes the mediator between men and God. There is a scene in the movie where we see him with a telephone to call Allah. He says,

"*Allah*'s been very busy lately. One side its independence. On the other side, Hindus and Muslims are fighting." (Film)

The group of men around Shanta always had a friendship with each other. But the partition turned the whole thing upside down. Even when they talk, the issue was partition. They started finding faults with other's religions. The Muslims make fun of Hindus and Sikhs. And vice versa. Muslims believe Sikhs are the fighting arms of Hindus and the Hindus are using Sikhs against them.

"Sikhs have a tradition of violence. Haven't you seen the paintings of their Gods? Holding severed hands dripping with blood" (Film)

Even though they started forming hatred over the others, there were a few who desired peace and love. Hassan was one among them. He tries to make his friends understand the necessity of unity. He is a man of light heart and thus cannot bear the upcoming riots between his friends. He makes his views to correct the views of the other Muslim friends who see Sikhs as the problem makers:

"Our Holy Koran lies in their Golden Temple in Amritsar. The Sikhs' faith came about to bring Hindus and Muslims closer. So why fight amongst friends?" (Film)

Almost the first half of the movie is about the events preceding Independence and partition. We can see Dil Navas and Shanta flying kites on the rooftop of Dil Navas' house. There are many people flying kites. This makes the impression that the people were actually not much aware of the upcoming riots. They were untouched by the political problems crouching their religion. They enjoy their life in merry-making. The bright colour of the kites represents the happiness in their lives. The scene of Shanta and Dil Navas flying kites is important. This is the scene where we see how attracted Dil Navas was to Shanta. They spend such an intimacy where we feel they are in love. But actually, Shanta was in love with Hassan, another Muslim among their group.

Partition did not mean two new geographical dominions. It also gives birth to two psychological dominions. Not only the physical partition of geographical areas but also the psychic partition of minds. As the movie moves to the night of Independence, we see the shift from a friendly atmosphere to that of hatred. The only important scene where we cannot see Lenny is the scene at the railway station where Dil Navas is waiting for the train from Gurdaspur. He was waiting for his sisters. When the train arrives, he runs to it and was shocked to see the corpses of people, especially Muslims. The train carried only the dead bodies of Muslims. Later Lenny learns this through the conversation with people. Lenny is not witnessing the things. She hears that there was a massacre, Muslims were butchered and four sacks of women's breasts were found on the train. The irony is that soon after the news of the riot is disclosed by a man, we hear the speech of Pandit Jawaharlal Nehru on the Independence. "At the stroke of the midnight hour of August 15, 1947, when the world sleeps, India will awake to life and freedom". The man from the group who listens to this responds to this by saying "These politicians speak with such twisted tongues. Some independence they give us soaked in our brother's blood."

A wide shift of Navas' character begins from the train scene. Even though he has a sort of strange behavior from the very beginning of the movie, his serene nature vanishes from this part. Once he had a good time making merry with Shanta. But later he witnesses the riots of the place from the same rooftop with Shanta,

Hassan, and Lenny. He wants revenge for the death of his sisters. He wants to kill Hindus and Sikhs for chopping off the breasts of his sisters. When the Muslim group burns the Sikh inhabited area, we see a trace of happiness, laughter, and satisfaction on the face of Navas. A beastly joy. And this frightens others. When Hassan runs out to help the people who are burned, Dil Navas approaches Shanta and talks out his mind, "It's not about Hindus and Muslims. It's about what's inside us. Hindus- Muslims- Sikhs. We are all bastards, all animals. Like the lion in the zoo that Lenny baby is so scared of. He just lies there, waiting for the cage to open. And when it does, then God helps us all." (Film)

He wants Shanta to be with him so that he can control the beast inside him. But Shanta rejects this proposal. Later, we see Dil Navas gifting a gold coin that he took from a Hindu money lender while attacking his home. Even this was a sort of proposal and Shanta rejects the coin too. Hassan was watching the whole event. Dil Navas was suspicious about their relationship and he comes to the conclusion that he was right. Later in the scene, he witnesses Hassan and Shanta making love. Lenny also peeps through the window and finds Shanta and Hassan making love. She also notices Dil Navas viewing all this. On the very next day, Hassan was found murdered and tied in a sack.

The condition of the nation and the inner splits among the people is depicted through the scene where we see Lenny tearing the doll. She, along with her friend tears the doll apart. Likewise, the whole nation was torn apart by the Dominion of India and the Dominion of Pakistan. There were conversions. Hindus in Lahore convert them to either Muslims or Christians. For them, Lahore was their native place and they could not shift to another place. The second last scene of the movie is where we see the Muslim group attacking the Parsees and asking for the Hindus who live there. There was only Shanta who was still a Hindu. The gardener Hari was converted to Himmat Ali, a Muslim and another servant became a Christian. The group was told that Shanta went to Amritsar. Dil Navas appears in the scene and plays his tactics with

Lenny and finds out that Shanta was hiding in her mother's bedroom. Dil Navas let his fellow beings know this. The scene ends with the group dragging Shanta out of the house and Lenny running to her *Ice Candy walla* to plead to leave Shanta. Dil Navas pulls his cart and moves away.

There is no mention of what happens to Shanta. She might have been raped and tortured. That was the fate of women during the time of partition and riots. Shanta is a representative of the women who were tortured and murdered.

Lenny becomes a substitute for India, the one with colorful dreams but shattered due to the events around her. The dream of Independent India was unity. But the nation was torn apart. There was no physical event like partition. The whole event is psychological. There is no distinction between countries as such on-mother Earth. The idea of making boundaries begins in the minds and the boundaries exist within minds. The feeling of belongingness to a place will remain inside the minds. The shatter will remain the same. To belong to a place where others see them as an import will give rise to consequent riots. And the whole bloodshed will continue like a cycle.

The trauma created by the partition and the loss of Ayah is evident in adult self of Lenny in the last scene of the movie.

"Two hundred and fifty years of British empire ended in1947, but what's there to show for it except the country divided? The massacres and kidnappings, vendettas, and more violence were it all worth it? Fifty years have gone by since I betrayed my Ayah. Some say she married Ice Candy Man. Some say they saw her in a brothel in Lahore. Some say they saw her in Amritsar. But I never set eyes on her again. And that day in 1947, when I lost Ayah, I lost a large part of myself."

This statement is the real cry of the refugees, the migrants of partition. The whole movie is a depiction by a filmmaker who holds the part of nobody. The movie supports no religion, no riots, and no massacres. But the only concern of the filmmaker is the trauma and psychological aspects of people. The minds of the suffered. The minds of the shattered. The mirror held against the real history of Indian independence. The Independence from the British was soaked in blood.

WORKS CITED

1947 *Earth*. Dir. Deepa Mehta, Perf. Rahul Khanna, Nandita Das, Maia Sethna, Aamir Khan.1998.

Vishwanath, Gita and Salma Malik. "Revisiting 1947 through Popular Cinema: A Comparative Study of India and Pakistan." *Economic and Political Weekly* 05 September 2009:61-67.

BIO - NOTE

Meriya George is a guest lecturer in Bharat Mata College Thrikkakkara. She completed her Bachelor's degree in English Language and Literature from St. Xavier's College for Women, Aluva under M G University, Master's degree in English Language and Literature from Sree Sankaracharya University of Sanskrit, Kalady, and B.Ed. Degree from Titus II Teachers College, Thiruvalla under M G University. Her areas of interest include Indian Literature in English, Indian Aesthetics and Mythology.

DEVELOPING ENGLISH SPEAKING SKILLS OF THE ENGINEERING STUDENTS THROUGH DRAMA AS TEACHING TECHNIQUE

V. Dorothy Catherine

Assistant Professor, Department of English

St. Mary's College (Autonomous), Thoothukudi.

ABSTRACT

Drama as a teaching technique has been adapted by language instructors across the globe. This research is intended to identify the impact that drama as a teaching technique has created in enhancing the speaking skills of Engineering students. Students pursuing Engineering degrees have been surveyed from Chennai, India. The three aspects with respect to speaking skills namely fluency, structure grammar, and pronunciation have been evaluated. The study also examines whether the relationship between the independent and dependent variables is moderated by the medium of instruction in which the student pursued his/her education at the school level. The outcome shows that pronunciation is the most influential factor over fluency and structure grammar through regression and ANOVA techniques. The results show that teaching through drama enhances the speaking skills of engineering students.

Keywords: Engineering students, Speaking skills, Drama as a teaching technique, English language proficiency, and Professional course.

Developing English Speaking Skills of The Engineering Students Through Drama as Teaching Technique

• • •

INTRODUCTION

Students' active participation in classroom activities is a troublesome question for many teachers, especially those ones who rely on more learner-centered methodology. But this becomes a challenge when students speaking skills matters a lot. People usually speak more than they actually write; consequently, speaking is as well possibly the primary aim for anyone pursuing education. However, it can be often hindered by various factors, for example, reticence, low self-confidence, fear of judgment, indolence, etc. In this context, drama activities are considered so effective tool and important in an academic context (Ulas, 2008). The first significant function linked with drama in education is advancing speaking skills. Regardless of the use of drama techniques in the classroom atmosphere is quite contemporary, it was originally utilized by other organizations as a teaching and as well instruction technique (Ashton-Hay, 2005). Amongst the various advantages of employing drama techniques in a classroom, Fabio, (2014) emphasized that they are entertaining, and enjoyable and contribute to motivating students' learning process.

A dramatization is an outstanding tool for learning speaking skills in a safe and reliable set of classrooms. In terms of drama techniques, learners are given specific roles to play. It makes them try to apply the tasks before they do a discussion or conversation in a real context. It offers a credible environment for learning practice where students are open to taking opportunities, posing different questions, and modifying topics in a small group or as a pair. Samantaray, (2014) specified that drama activities assist students to utilize their language and other skills by means of these real-life activities. As Demircioglu (2010) suggests, in this technique the student is both player and observer, playing a role whilst communicating with others in a given role. Samantaray, (2014) emphasized that drama activities offer learners an extensive range of contextualized and scaffolding activities that progressively entail more contribution and more language proficiency, they are as well nonthreatening and hold no end of fun

Students' contribution to the entire learning process has turned out to be the main objective of contemporary approaches which focus on learner-centered classes instead of a teacher-centered classroom setting. Clever involvement which claims a student to utilize analytical or creative thinking skills is the type of contribution which makes students to learn efficiently. Drama is obviously proven to be one of the most significant techniques which provide much more contribution for both learners in the learning process. Mattevi (2005) specified the usage of drama in the classroom lets the teachers to exhibit the target language in a dynamic, interactive, and contextualized way. Dramatization supports the teacher adopt different skills, such as speaking, writing, reading, etc. Albalawi, (2014) emphasized that drama empowers students, in the overall education process, to improve their communicative skills for example creativity, problem-solving, analytical skill, and socialization and it gives students the opportunity for self-exploration and teamwork.

When using drama techniques like role plays, lateral thinking, dialogues, conversations, etc. students are more likely to have the opportunity to employ language to manage and respond to various real situations, self-consciously building their knowledge of the actual world and improving their capability to communicate with other people. When drama performances are employed in the EFL setting, the instructor becomes a learning catalyst, in charge of developing a systematized and coordinated environment, setting objectives, defining groups and offering students their roles, choosing materials and allocating time for each task. Conejero and Fernandes (2009) reported that in a fun-based learning atmosphere, students will feel contented and confident, which ultimately improves their readiness of learning.

One of the main qualities of the social aspect of speaking skills is the capability to communicate a thought comfortably and also with confidence. In such cases, drama can be considered the ideal technique for students to build self-confidence (Lucia, 2007). Drama can promote language skills including reading, speaking, and paying attention by developing a suitable context. Drama is an influential teaching tool that entails all of the students to interact efficiently. Drama techniques could also offer the means for linking up students' emotions and reasoning since it empowers students to take chances with speaking abilities and experience the relationship between thought and action (Maley, 2005). Zyoud, (2010) emphasized that drama is considered an efficient tool for teaching pronunciation since different components such as non-verbal communication and intonation could be practiced in a combined way.

This study focuses upon the variables, a) the dependent variable being the drama as a teaching technique to the engineering students (DV) and b) the independent variable being 'speaking skills' (with constructs fluency, structure grammar, and pronunciation) and how the moderator "medium of instruction at school level" impacts the proposed variables.

LITERATURE REVIEW

1. Introduction

Oradee, (2012) studied the role of drama techniques in classroom settings. The study examined the role of developing speaking skills through drama techniques, i.e., role-playing. Drama education is an influential teaching and learning technique with intense positive impacts on students' cognitive, psychological, and physical development. The study reported that drama techniques enhance students' writing, speaking, and imaginative expression. In line with the current study, it is clear that speaking skills could be enhanced through communicative activities, i.e. a role-playing method. Besides, drama techniques could motivate the learners and develop positive relationships between the educator and the students and also amongst the students, thus boosting a supportive atmosphere for language learning.

Qureshi, (2016) brings to light, the significance of students' speaking skills. The study employs a communicative method for the improvement of the speaking skills of students in the classroom setting. The study focuses on the problem of learners who are intrinsically capable but could not communicate properly. The study also pays attention to the processes entailed in the communicative process of the students, thus carrying out such activities in the classroom which empower students to be capable to employ the language suitable to a given social perspective. Students' speaking skills help them to converse with others, to convey their ideas, and to understand others' thoughts and ideas as well. As the study's findings reported without speech, any communicative language will be reduced to a mere character.

Atas, (2014) expressed that action is a significant part of the learning process since it entails body language and motivation and it also keeps students engaged in the learning process. While making an effort to figure out if drama contributes positively to students' speaking skills development, the current study has also emphasized that drama reduces the anxiety levels of EFL learning students. In drama, there will be both emotion and movement, in which these two have the power for delivering verbal skills. Amongst all the positive influences of drama in another learning sequence, the development of speaking skills has a very exceptional place. The drama keeps learners energetic in the learning process. It also positively contributes to students' self-confidence and motivation. Language games, role play, lateral thinking, and scripts are some of the drama techniques employed in the current study. After six consecutive weeks of usage of drama training, the study emphasized that drama techniques considerably reduce the speaking anxiety of students.

The hypothesis H1 is formulated as:

H1: Drama as a teaching technique enhances the pronunciation skill of engineering students while speaking English;

2.2 Increasing fluency and structure grammar through drama techniques

Ampatuan and Jose (2016) expressed that fluency is basically linked to students' control over their verbal knowledge. This study puts forward that speech fluency is a multi-dimensional concept wherein different sub-dimensions could be differentiated, for example, speed fluency, breakdown fluency, and repair fluency. This research puts forward that more should be achieved to enhance oral fluency. As an important category of communicative activity, role-play contributes to helping the learners to have an expressive and inclusive interaction and gives a chance to practice fluency whilst using the English language. Respondents of the study believe that their teacher exercises the role-play activity in their classroom by fostering them to speak the language with increased fluency. The study also reported that role-play activities help to encourage students in such a way that they express themselves; provide self-confidence and a chance for applying the rules of social behavior, and empower students to practice their learned language effectively.

Kuśnierek, (2015) emphasized that role-playing positively contributes to developing learners' fluency in speaking. Currently, many people find fluency in speaking ability with the most appropriate competence in their target language, for being capable of talking effortlessly with a native speaker more frequently shows the actual linguistic level. The author emphasized that activities that exercise connected speech, instead of activities concentrated only on specific phonemes, enhance students' fluency. The study also reported that role-play has a significant role in developing speaking skills. The findings of the study clearly exhibited that using role-play activities improves students' speaking skills, particularly fluency and pronunciation. The respondents put forward that drama techniques seem more appealing to them since it is amusing to perform someone else's role. The students also accentuated that they felt that their fluency level is gradually increased after employing drama techniques.

Thus, hypothesis H2 is formulated as:

H2: Drama as a teaching technique enhances the fluency skill of engineering students while speaking English;

The research by Benabadji, (2007) dealt with adult learners and the reason for their difficulty level in speaking skills. Students usually attend school or college not only to study the subject matter; but also, to enhance their speaking skills and fluency. One of the challenges experienced by learners apart from their acquirement of grammatical structures and pronunciation is their speaking skills. Accordingly, this study adopts the usage of drama activities for example role-play activity which helps improve the students" speaking skills, particularly their fluency level. In this research, it is evidently exhibited through the data gathered that role-play plays an important role in the development of the student's communication skills. The findings also reported that role-playing employed in the classroom setting could positively contribute to improving the fluency level of students.

Drama techniques empower students to learn the verbal and as well non-verbal language, such as intonation and pronunciation. Vocabulary and grammar structures are staged and practiced through drama techniques. They are usually supplemented by the usage of body language. As stated by Billíková and Kissova (2013) just grammar, and vocabulary, but as well pronunciation, fluency, intonation, etc. are taught effortlessly, and teaching these characteristics of language is poorly ignored in traditional classrooms, which can be included through drama techniques.

Thus, hypothesis H3 is formulated as:

H3: Drama as a teaching technique enhances the structure and grammar skills of the engineering students while speaking English;

2.3 Medium of instructions

The authors Galante and Thomson studied upon the instructional approaches of Drama as technique over fluency, accent and comprehensibility of the students and how effective the drama influences the students. According to findings and outcomes from the study by the authors, the enhancement of speaking skills in schools and colleges are done through drama and other teaching techniques where the students learn to communicate fluently through games, fun activities, events and role-plays. Drama as techniques in the teaching practices has been found by the authors to be effective than the traditional teaching tools. The teaching techniques might vary from one-individual to another yet the communication of the information from the teacher to learner should be through a formal mode where the students will learn to understand the concept with structure grammar, vocabulary and comprehension.

The authors Walan and Enochsson (2019) examined about the potential of utilizing the storytelling combined with drama as a learning tool among the younger children of 4-8years with 25sample as the size. They found that, drama along with role-playing and storytelling influences and impacts the learners through audio (sensory learning) as medium of instruction than showing pictures or story boards. According to study's outcomes, it's understandable that drama is a medium of instruction (also-known-as: instructional strategy) in teaching, where the learners (students) show interest to develop their skill and fact adaption.

The author Kondal (2016) explored the Drama as a must needed tool/ technique in teaching to integrate the skills with the individual's language. The findings of study confirmed that, drama as a stimulus to learners, certainly and evidently impacts them with developing their fluency where it acts as an instructional strategy that assists the individuals as a "medium". The conclusion portrayed those practical methods like drama enacting, role-playing, skits and more has higher impact than theoretical practices.

Alasmari and Alshae'el (2020) studied the impact of adopting drama as a technique in English-language learning with learners of age group 10-12years in Saudi based two primary schools with 40samples. The findings offered the researchers with facts and outcomes that language acquisition through dramatization is positively possible among young learners where they can improve their vocabulary, grammar, comprehension, fluency and pronunciation. However, there are findings that stated that children who felt uncomfortable in communicating detached from role-playing, mimes, dramas and skits thinking that they would undergo embarrassment, interference and inhibition; authors concluded that the challenges should be met with solutions and perseverance with reliable and regular more practices.

Masoumi-Moghaddam (2018) argued through his analyses that drama and drama-based tools in learning/ teaching the English language, especially with foreign language learners, certainly eradicate MTI where pronunciation plays a vital role with a 'neutral accent'. Also, to improve one's grammar and its structure, the verbal lessons through role-playing and skits (dramatization techniques) are found to be more effective than traditional teaching techniques and tools.

Thus, hypotheses H4-H6 where the moderator impacts the variables are formulated as:

H4: The enhancement of English pronunciation skill of the Engineering students on employing drama as a teaching technique is independent of the medium of instructions of the students at school level;

H5: The enhancement of English fluency skill of the Engineering students on employing drama as a teaching technique is independent of the medium of instructions of the students at school level;

H6: The enhancement of English structure grammar skill of the Engineering students on employing drama as a teaching technique is independent of the medium of instructions of the students at school level.

4. Teachers' perception towards using role-playing in classroom

Anissa and Azis (2014) studied students and teachers' perceptions towards the efficiency of employing drama techniques in classroom context. The study also explored students' feedback on the advantage of drama-based movements to their motive to learn, self-confidence and anxiety. The findings indicate that mainstream of the teachers feel that drama performances are efficient since it helps enhance their motivation to learn, intensify their level of confidence and lessen their language anxiety. The students' insight has been supported by teachers' perspective which really favours the application of drama techniques and has provided their acknowledgement on the efficiency of the applying drama-based techniques in the classroom setting. The finding emphasized that both students and teachers adopt the concept of the efficiency of applying drama techniques in classroom since it benefits learners not only with regards to academic but it as well plays an important role in learners' affective development.

Cerkez, et al (2012) aimed to explore the perspective of teachers in role playing and other drama techniques. Self-report has been used in the current study. Besides, thematic analysis has been employed to assess qualitative data on the basis of key subject. The place of drama and role playing has influence to follow future professional experience. Drama and role playing has a significant role to encourage awareness of future teaching practice and also on account of team work and communication within small groups. The findings reported that drama and role-playing activities in education provide reflection, discussion, communication and team work skills. Besides, this learning environment fosters pedagogical and as well practical knowledge. To conclude, the teacher respondents of the current study emphasized that drama and role playing can be considered an efficient learning tool for the students in which they can gain self-confidence and develop friendship bonds with others.

2.5 Theoretical framework

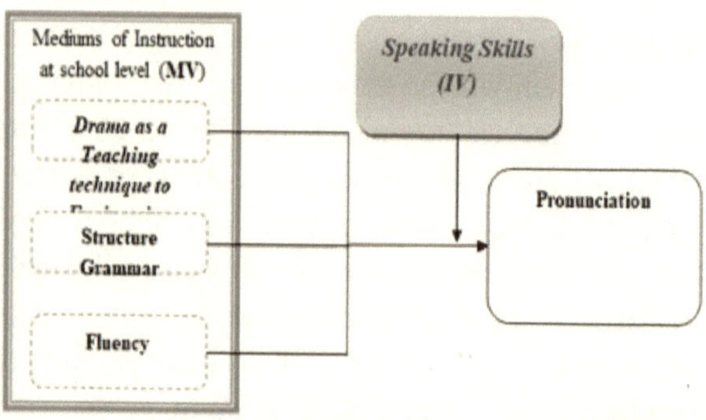

Figure 1 Conceptual Framework (Source: Author)

The theoretical framework (fig 1) of the research comprises independent variables where the speaking skill sets comprising factors pronunciation, structure grammar and fluency with the 'drama as teaching technique' being the dependent variable being moderated by the medium of instructions.

Hypotheses:

H1: Drama as a teaching technique enhances the pronunciation skill of the engineering students while speaking English;

H2: Drama as a teaching technique enhances the fluency skill of the engineering students while speaking English;

H3: Drama as a teaching technique enhances the structure grammar skill of the engineering students while speaking English;

H4: The enhancement of English pronunciation skill of the Engineering students on employing drama as a teaching technique is independent of the medium of instructions of the students at school level;

H5: The enhancement of English fluency skill of the Engineering students on employing drama as a teaching technique is independent of the medium of instructions of the students at school level;

H6: The enhancement of English structure grammar skill of the Engineering students on employing drama as a teaching technique is independent of the medium of instructions of the students at school level.

1. *RESEARCH METHODOLOGIES*

The research follows the quantitative approach since it attempts to examine the facts and information towards the formulated hypothesis and evaluates the outcomes through numerical analyses.

3.1. Data collection

Data is vital and yet also the most essential source in a research/study where the researcher has to focus on two resources: primary (collected by investigator) and secondary (pre-gathered data relevant to the topic). The research being a quantitative one and examines the medium of instruction as moderating factor collects data through both sources; where the primary information (data) is acquired through closed-end questionnaire (survey) and secondary resources are gathered from journals, articles, researches,
web-based reliable articles, etc. In the research, the engineering students are focused as the targets where the sampling size is *n=216.* The research had adopted the simple random sampling technique where each variable and the factors involved will gain a chance of being evaluated. The study adopts the Regression methods, ANOVA, Moderation Analysis (where the moderator's impact is examined) and the software utilized are SPSS and Microsoft packages.

The instrument here is framed as a closed-end questionnaire adopted from the study developed by Zahara (2018) with 25items in independent variables and 15items in dependent variables. In this study the relevant items (pronunciation, structure grammar and fluency) and the teaching through drama are alone considered as the constructs for the research where, the constructs involved are:

1. TTD (15),
2. SKSG (5);
3. SKP (5) and
4. SKF (5).

The 15-TTD items along with 15-SK items had been adopt by Rao (2019) in his research where he examined the importance and efficiency of the speaking skills in English language and the constructs, variables and analyses were found to be reliable; thus, the research also adopts the above-mentioned constructs in this study.

1. *RESULTS, FINDINGS AND HYPOTHESIS TESTING*

4.1 Result

The research obtained outcomes where the result showed that independent variables: *pronunciation, structure grammar and fluency certainly enhance the dependent variable TTD* (Teaching-Through-Drama) amongst the Engineering students' English speaking. The multiple regression analysis and the ANOVA tests upon the variables have been estimated in this research. R, Adjusted R-square and R-square values of regression have been calculated to insert as input for the ANOVA to obtain mean square, frequency and significant value to verify whether the ANOVA is insignificant / significant based on the outcome of 'sig'. The outcomes of the analyses are:

Descriptive Statistics			
	Mean	*Std. Deviation*	*N*
TTDMEAN	3.7060	.59993	216
MEANSKP	2.8991	.75796	216
MEANSKPSG	2.7287	.71704	216
MEANSKF	3.5389	.79858	216

Table 1 REGRESSION ANALYSIS

Model	R	R Square	Adjusted R Square	Std. Error of the Estimate	Change Statistics				
					R Square Change	F Change	df1	df2	Sig. F Change
1	.681[a]	.463	.451	.44464	.463	36.280	5	210	.000

a. Predictors: (Constant), MEANSKPSG, MEANSKF, MEANSKP

b. Dependent Variable: TTDMEAN

Table 2 REGRESSION MODEL SUMMARY

ANOVA[a]					
Model		Sum of Squares	Df	Mean Square	F	Sig.
1	Regression	35.864	5	7.173	36.280	.000[b]
	Residual	41.518	210	.198		
	Total	77.382	215			

a. Dependent Variable: TTDMEAN

b. Predictors: (Constant), MEANSKPSG, MEANSKF, MEANSKP

The outcomes through ANOVA are found as "significant".

Coefficients					
Model	Un-standardized Coefficients		Standardized Coefficients	t	Sig.
	B	Std. Error	Beta		
1 (Constant)	.848	.254		3.344	.001
MEANSKP	.105	.051	.133	2.046	.042
MEANSKPSG	-.051	.048	-.061	-1.068	.287
MEANSKV	.736	.076	.660	9.723	.000
MEANSKF	-.036	.052	-.048	-.685	.494
MEANSKC	-.013	.040	-.017	-.336	.738
a. Dependent Variable: TTDMEAN					

Table 4 OUTCOMES OF ANOVA

4.2 Findings

Based on the outputs the findings were obtained. Table 5 below represents the variable validation values under the Cronbach alpha testing method. Prior data analyses and evaluation researchers had to validate each construct individually where the alpha score should be higher than 0.6.

S. No	Construct	Item	Alpha
1	Teaching through drama	15	.948
2	Pronunciation	5	.889
3	Fluency	5	.921
4	Structure Grammar	5	.785

Table 5 CONSTRUCT VALIDATION

From the table, it is clear and understandable that all four constructs have scores higher than 0.750 which shows that the constructs involved are valid and efficient for the study

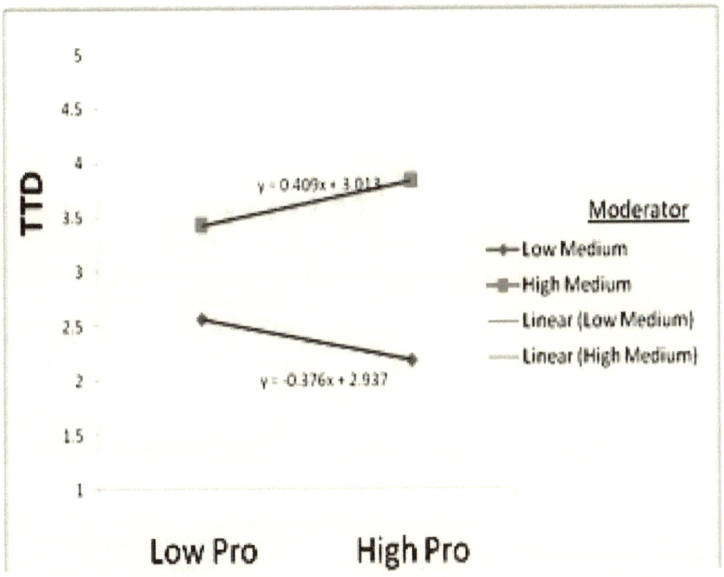

Figure 2: Interaction Graph-plot of TTD and Pronunciation

Inference: Figure (2) shows that, there exists a positive relationship between the variables TTD (Teaching-Through-Drama) and SKP (Skill Pronunciation) where the medium of instructions as moderator strengthens the relationship. The interaction effect through the analysis of the moderator between the variables TTD and SKP is found as .1966.

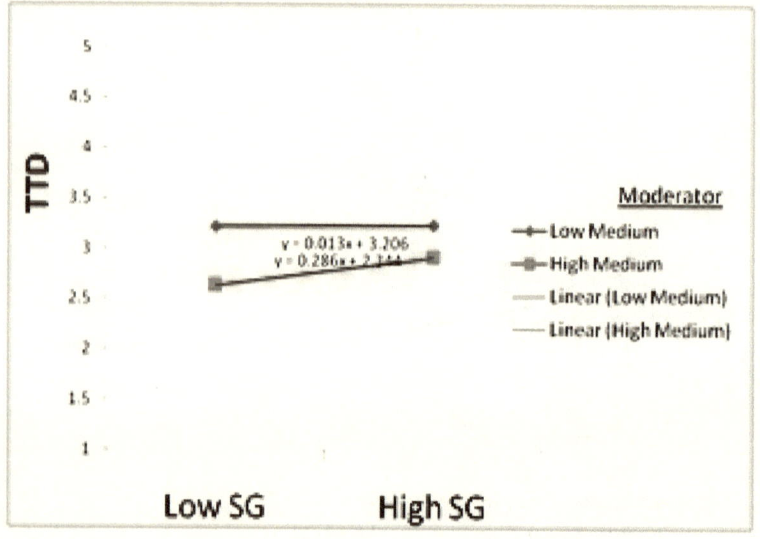

Figure 3: Interaction Graph-plot of TTD and Structure Grammar

Inference: Figure (3) shows that, there exists a positive relationship between the variables TTD (Teaching-Through-Drama) and SG (Structure Grammar) where the medium of instructions as moderator strengthens the relationship. The interaction effect through the analysis of the moderator between the variables TTD and SKSG is found as .0681.

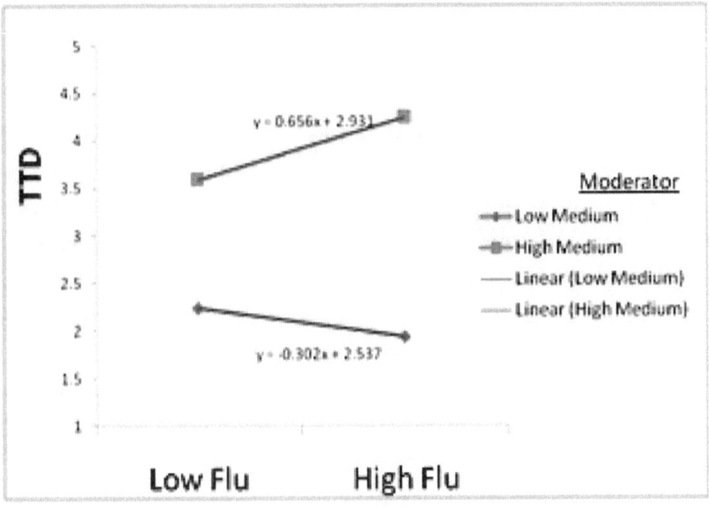

Figure 4: Interaction Graph-plot of TTD and Fluency

Inference: Figure (4) shows that, there exists a positive relationship between the variables TTD (Teaching-Through-Drama) and SKP (Skill Fluency) where the medium of instructions as moderator strengthens the relationship. The interaction effect through the analysis of the moderator between the variables TTD and SKF is found as .2398.

4.3 Hypothesis Testing

Hypothesis

1. Drama as a teaching technique enhances the pronunciation skill of the engineering students while speaking English - **Accepted**

2. Drama as a teaching technique enhances the fluency skill of the engineering students while speaking English - **Accepted**

3. Drama as a teaching technique enhances the structure and grammar skill of the engineering students while speaking English - **Accepted**

4. The enhancement of English pronunciation skills of the Engineering students on employing drama as a teaching technique

is independent of the medium of instruction of the students at the school level - **Accepted**

5. The enhancement of English fluency skill of the Engineering students on employing drama as a teaching technique is independent of the medium of instruction of the students at school level - **Accepted**

6. The enhancement of English structure grammar skill of the Engineering students on employing drama as a teaching technique is independent of the medium of instruction of the students at the school level - **Accepted**

The table 6 represents that the formulated hypothesis based upon the independent (SKP, SKSG and SKF) and dependent (TTD) variables are moderated by the "medium of instructions" as the moderating variable in the research.

5. DISCUSSION AND CONCLUSION

Through the research analysis it is found that, dramatization as a teaching technique/ tool among the young learners (school and college students) are quite effective where it influences their structure grammar, fluency and pronunciation. The independent variables: fluency, structure grammar and pronunciation of the factor "speaking skills" have been analysed with the moderator "medium of instructions" where it influence and enhances the students' speaking skills in English language. As per the outcomes and the results, the findings portrayed that, pronunciation is the most influential variable than the variables fluency and structure grammar, respectively. The outcomes of the pronunciation shows higher impact than the fluency and structure grammar implying that drama as tool/ technique in teaching impacts student's accent than fluency and grammar correction.

The study analysed and examined the Engineering student's speaking skills where the pronunciation is found to be more effective than fluency and structure grammar through dramatization as a teaching tool.

WORKS CITED

Alasmari. N and Alshae'el. A, (2020), "The Effect of Using Drama in English Language Learning among Young Learners: A Case Study of 6th Grade Female Pupils in Sakaka City", *International Journal of Education & Literacy Studies,* 8(1), 61-73.

Albalawi, B.R. (2014). Effectiveness of Teaching English Subject using Drama on the Development of Students' Creative Thinking. *IOSR Journal of Research & Method in Education (IOSR-JRME),* 4(6), pp. 54-63.

Ameri, G. A., & Nezakat-Alhosseini, M. (2017). Long Term effects of collaborative task planning vs. individual task planning on Persian – speaking EFL learners' writing performance. *Journal of Research in Applied Linguistics,* 8(1), pp. 146-164.

Ampatuan, R.A., Jose, A.E.S. (2016). Role Play as an Approach in Developing Students' Communicative Competence. *International Educative Research Foundation and Publisher,* pp. 18-24.

Ashton-Hay, S. (2005). Drama: Engaging all Learning Styles. Proceedings 9th International INGED (Turkish English Educational Association) Conference. Economics and Technical University in Ankara, Turkey.

Atas, M. (2014). The reduction of speaking anxiety in EFL learners through drama techniques. *Procedia - Social and Behavioral Sciences,* volume 176, pp. 961 – 969.

Azis, A, Anissa, N. (2014). A study on the effectiveness of using drama techniques in teaching English: Trainee teachers and students' perspectives. Retrieved on 4th May 2021 from https://ir.uitm.edu.my/id/eprint/14648/

Barbu, Lucia (2007) Using Drama techniques for teaching English. As Cited in Zyoud, M. (2010). Using Drama Activities and Techniques to Foster Teaching English as a Foreign Language: a Theoretical Perspective. Researchgate Publications.

Benabadji, S. (2007). Improving Students' Fluency through Role-Playing. Master Thesis, Degree of Magister in Educational Psychology.

Billíková, A, Kissova, M. (2013). Drama Techniques in the Foreign Language Classroom. Academia Publications.

Carrasco, V, Dinapoli, R. (2012). Engaging in Dramatic Activites in English as a Foreign Language

Classes at the University Level. *Encuentro*, volume 21, pp. 94-103.

Cerkez, Y, Altinay, X, Altinay, F, Bashirova, E. (2012). Drama and Role Playing in Teaching

Practice: The Role of Group Works. *Journal of Education and Learning*, 1(2), pp. 109-120.

Conejero, A.L., Fernandes, A.O.D.Z. (2009) Efficiency And Effectiveness Of Drama Techniques In The English Classroom. International Congress of the Association of Young Linguists.

Fabio, T. (2014). Drama techniques to enhance speaking skills and motivation in the EFL secondary classroom. Retrieved on 29th April 2021 from

Housen, A., &Kuiken, F. (2009). Complexity, accuracy, and fluency in second language acquisition. *Appl. Linguist.*, 30(4), pp. 461-473.

Kondal.B. (2016), "Drama as a teaching tool for the integration of language skills". *Veda's Journal of English Language and Literature-JOELL*, 3(2), 92-98.

Kuśnierek, A. (2015). Developing students' speaking skills through role-play. *World Scientific News*, volume 1, pp. 73-111.

Lapaire, J. R. (2006). English Grammar in Motion. Paris, France: Editions Hachette.

Masoumi-Moghaddam, S. (2018). Using Drama and Drama Techniques to Teach English Conversations to English as a Foreign Language Learners. *International Journal of Applied Linguistics and English Literature*, 7(6), pp. 63-68.

CHAPTER VI

COLONIAL GAZE: DECONSTRUCTING STEREOTYPICAL INDIAN LEADS FROM THE NETFLIX SHOW BRIDGERTON

Ameya Mary Yovakim
Assistant Professor in English
St. Aloysius College, Edathua

ABSTRACT

Indian representations in Western movies have always been limited to the so-called 'brown identity'. These brown-skinned characters often fall prey to colonial stereotypes and appropriation. Most popular and critically acclaimed films about the east by the west have always been entrapped in the meshes of colonial stereotypes and have always been looked through the monotonous shades of the colonial gaze. Western representation of Indians in literature and movies has always ended in clichés and stereotypes as shy nerds or reliable sidekicks. Popular Netflix shows like 'Never Have I Ever and 'Bridgerton experiment with Indian lead characters. However, despite the myriad attempt to integrate multi-ethnic features into the series, the creators of the 'Bridgerton' have stumbled many times at stereotyping the third-world characters.
Keywords: Colonial Stereotype, Clichés, Appropriation, Ethnicity, and Culture.

Colonial Gaze: Deconstructing Stereotypical Indian Leads From the Netflix Show *Bridgerton*

• • •

Stereotypes arise when self-integration is threatened. They are therefore part of our own way of dealing with the instabilities of our perception of the world. This is not to say that they are good, only that they are necessary (Gilman 18).

From time immemorial, stereotypes are used rather unconsciously as strategies of orientation and identity find; and only in a subsequent phase, they are exploited for additional purposes, for instance, the merging of power in imperial structures. In Roland Barthe's explanation of contemporary myth, he considers that images and words are equally responsible for generating texts of mythological weight. He claims that the apparatus of myth establishes, renders harmless, and legitimates social constructions. Mythic discourse unvaryingly reduces things to the bareness of essences or stereotypes, and 'freezes into an eternal reference' that which it wishes to justify (Barthes, 7). The 'white mythology' of colonial discourse is an example of a text that merges and encodes legitimating myths or meta-narratives.

Although stereotypes are not entirely created in group contexts, most theorists agree that they are particularly endorsed by people who define themselves as members of a certain group in order to place themselves against people who are outside this group. Stereotypes can be transformed into dangerous prejudices whenever the group order is threatened by the 'other' or polar group. In contrast to stereotypes, which function chiefly as an aid to orientation, prejudices are thus created to propose not only external factors of otherness to the outside group but also attribute internal and unchangeable reasons for their otherness (Grin).

In the case of the British Raj, however, most critics are reluctant to confirm 'prejudices' as the defining factor of the relationships between colonizer and colonized, although most of them identify stereotyping as "crucial in the colonial system" (Grin). It becomes reasonable that some Europeans, like the early Orientalist Friedrich Max Müller, believed in a historically shared Aryan background of Europeans and Indians, but at the same time stated that the contemporary condition of Indians was regressive, and a very different one from Europeans.

Indians and Europeans shared a common heritage, but for Max Müller their contemporary position was fundamentally different. He believed that Europeans had continued to build upon the high achievements of their Aryan ancestors, while Indian culture had become stagnant, even degenerate (Ballantyne: 43).

The idealistic view of the Orient, during the past times, is still a misrepresentation, even if driven at times by respect for the Orient. These falsified and romantic idealizations of the orient and the projection of stereotypical forms ultimately aim for domestication and control of the East (King: 92).

But what primarily seems rather surprising, if not illogical, can be explained when one considers the stereotype as a "form of splitting and multiple belief" (Bhabha, 77) which "requires, for its successful signification, a continual and repetitive chain of other stereotypes" (77). For Homi Bhabha, stereotypes are to be regarded as 'impossible objects' (81) which represent both the demand to expel and the desire to explore the unknown and thus functioning both as phobia and fetish with respect to the colonizers (72-73).

However, the creation of new stereotypes during a crucial point does not automatically lead to the erasure of those images but leads to an ongoing struggle with older clichés. In fact, the process of stereotyping can be described as a layering of new images over old ones without fully concealing those older pictures - a phenomenon that may produce inconsistent and contradicting images while serving the same purpose: the 'othering' of extremely different strangers. The stereotyped 'other' in colonial discourses is therefore never a uniform being but a "historical palimpsest which combined different and changing ways of characterizing the alien condition" (Grin).

The Netflix adaptation of Julia Quinn's popular Bridgerton novel series was made popular because of the colour-blind regency era, and the diversity of its cast - in this fantastical interpretation of the Regency period, whiteness is not a requirement for nobility, and race is merely a trait that characters are born with and destined to live, not one that defines their entire identity and existence. Though the Bridgertons, the upper-class and respected family around whom the story revolves around, is entirely white, prominent characters of colour abound. The first season alone features several leading Black characters, including the main male lead who happens to be the Duke of Hastings, an opinionated and sagacious witty dowager and the Queen of England, played by Regé Jean Page, Adjoa Andoh, and Golda Rosheuvel, respectively. The show employed 'color-conscious casting', which is defined as casting [that] intentionally considers the race and ethnicity of actors and the characters they play in order to oppose racism, honor and respect cultures, foster stronger productions, and contribute to a more equitable world.

The show's creator and executive producer, Chris Van Dusen, explained that this emphasis on colour consciousness was a way for him to recreate the Regency period in a way that reflected the multi-ethnic world we inhabit today. Van Dusen argues that he wanted to turn the period genre on its head and reimagine it in a new and exciting way; one that included characters of different colours and backgrounds; one that explored the topic of race. He also writes about his intention to include all the minorities existing in the universe. Van Dusen's attempt at a universe of debauched romance tropes that is largely colour-blind is successful to a greater degree as it is a globally most-watched Netflix series. However, with the airing of the second season of Bridgerton confronts this lack of context head-on by featuring the daughters of an Indian family, the Sharmas, as the central love interests of Anthony Bridgerton (played by Johnathon Bailey) in a passionate love triangle, unlike the Julia Quinn novel series. The Sharmas have returned to London decades after the Sharma sisters' mother, Lady Mary Sharma, (Shelley Conn) fell in love with a low-class Indian clerk, was disowned by her parents, and moved to Mumbai. Kate Sharma (Simone Ashley) is the clerk's daughter from a previous marriage and the overprotective older sister to Edwina Sharma (Charithra Chandran).

The girls' father passes away long before the Sharma women arrive in London, leaving the family nearly penniless. In order to reclaim some of Lady Mary's parents' fortune, Kate sets on a mission to betroth her sister to the English nobility in London.

The greatest criticism that arose against the second season of "Bridgerton" is its cultural inaccuracies. Most popular and critically acclaimed films about the east by the west have always been entrapped in the meshes of colonial stereotypes and have always been looked through the monotonous shades of the colonial gaze. Western representation of Indians in movies has always ended in clichés and stereotypes as shy nerds or reliable sidekicks. Popular Netflix shows like Never Have I Ever and Bridgerton experiment with Indian lead characters. Actor and writer Mindy Kaling, who made The Mindy Project and the Netflix hit Never Have I Ever, has been one of the most visible entertainment industry figures trying to expand the space for Indian-origin creators - and stories about their identity. Comedians such as Lilly Singh, Hasan Minhaj, and Hari Kondabolu, even brought the Indian-American/Canadian experience into the comedy scene and political satire.

Both lead actresses in Season 2 of the Bridgerton series are of Tamil origin and darker skinned — which is a feat of Indian diversity to be extolled and of itself, as colorism and stereotyping in the Indian Film Industry has often stripped darker-skinned and South Asian actresses of lead roles — and refer to their late father as "Appa", but the references to South Indian culture end there. Their father's last name is Sharma, which is a name that hails from North India. The girls speak Marathi and Hindi languages in which the word for father is not "Appa". They have lived in Mumbai for most of their lives which is entirely unrelated to the south Indian language and culture. Even their affectionate names for each other are a source of confusion - Edwina uses the Hindi word for older sister, "Didi", to refer to Kate, but Kate calls Edwina "Bon", which means younger sister in Bengali, which is a totally different language used in a totally different part of India. Colonial depiction of India has always side-lined the multi-ethnic characteristic of India. The Indian subcontinent is vastly around 1.7 million square miles, home to twenty-nine states, twenty-two official languages (and a far greater number of dialects), and countless cultures and traditions. But these traditions are different in different places.

Perhaps the strange amalgam of Indian culture that makes up Edwina and Kate might be an attempt to represent all Indians in one fell swoop.

Van Dusen's quest to create a 'multi-ethnic' period should have included the prerequisite of accuracy. Van Dusen does accomplish his goal to a degree, specifically by creating a world in which Edwina and Kate are admired as the most beautiful women in the city, where their Indian culture is woven into their interactions and characterization without being Westernized and where they are allowed to exist as Indians second and characters first, without their Indianness defining who they are completely or embodying easy stereotypes. (Anushka) Edwina Sharma asks her suitor Lord Bridgerton "Have you read Ghaleeb?" (00:36:12 -- 00:36:13 Bridgerton S2E3) in the episode 'A Bee in your Bonnet' (E02). The mention of Mirza Ghalib, a celebrated 19th Century Urdu poet, was one of the show's many attempts to emphasize the Indian origins of the heroines, Kate and Edwina Sharma, played by British-Indian actors Simone Ashley and Charithra Chandran, respectively. However, despite the myriad attempt to integrate multi-ethnic features into the series the creators of the Bridgertons have stumbled many times at stereotyping the third-world characters.

Western depiction of India always dealt with 'clashes of civilizations' where Western characters "saved" India from ancient religious practices of dubious sorcery, natural disasters such as floods and epidemics, as well as social injustices such as sati and poverty. On the other hand, there has also been a tendency to depict India in a dream-like, utopian manner where India is often represented as the land of milk and honey where overindulgences, excesses, and vices are an integral part of the culture (Ramasubramanian). But despite, or perhaps because, of the references - bangles, Indian-ish embroidery, masala chai, a melodramatic tune from the Bollywood blockbuster Kabhi Khushi Kabhi Gham, even a Hindu wedding tradition of Haldi ceremony-Bridgerton has raised a fair number of mocking eyebrows (Bridgerton S02E06).

Even the scene where Kate brews herself a cup of masala chai drew criticism. It was unsettling to see so many references to a beverage that traced its origins to the exploitation of tea plantation workers in India during British rule. The cultural and ethnic traces in the series range from the jewelry, to the Haldi ceremony, the hair oil massage, to the music, the cardamom tea, the use of Kate's full name at the end of the show, and the slight change in accent when the sisters speak to each other compared to when they speak to someone who is British has been able to attract the attention of the masses. However, these seemingly positive stereotypes not only fail to depict the multi-ethnicity of India but tagged India as pre-civilized, uncouth, and even entangled in meaningless traditions. Bridgerton's stylized, romantic take on Regency Britain has won fans, even grudging ones. Even in the first season, which featured a black duke as its hero, it did not really delve into the history of the hero, avoiding any mention of slavery or race. It does the same in its second season, where it tells the story of an Indian family visiting London to find an aristocratic match for their youngest daughter. They have arrived from Bombay but we know little else about their life in India.

Costume period dramas are expected to be the least historically accurate but there is something deeply malicious about creating a past that is utterly devoid of enslavement, empire, and genocide and the repercussions of those continue to harm (and kill) people today. Bridgerton is happy to cross-examine patriarchy but not the possible tensions between its characters who are black, brown, and white. But the colour of skin, which the show ignores as the propaganda to re-establish the multi-cultural, multi-ethnic modernized society, is hard to ignore in the viewing experience. It is ironic and impossible for a brown audience to watch a white grandfather tower over his brown granddaughter, screaming he will disinherit her, and to blindly accept that this power equation is merely sexist. It is hard not to think of the notions of purity built into Hinduism's unyielding caste system when you see a brown mother scorning her daughter for 'polluting' the family with her love affair, especially since the man she eloped with was not from the aristocracy. Since ignorance is blissful, the colour-blind regency era has been a seemingly perfect utopia. "Bridgerton's alternative reality is a place where people of colour can exist and experience love and joy and complicated relationships without the trauma that history brings of oppression, colonialism, and racism" (Sebastian).

WORKS CITED

Gilman, Sander L. "Why and How I Study German." The German Quarterly, vol. 62, no. 2, 1989, pp. 192–204. JSTOR, https://doi.org/10.2307/407371. Accessed 27 Sep. 2022.

Ballantyne, Tony. Orientalism and Race: Aryanism in the British Empire, Palgrave Macmillan. 2006. Barthes, Roland. Mythologies: Roland Barthes. Hill and Wang, 1972

King, Richard. "Orientalism and the Modern Myth of 'Hinduism.'" Numen, vol. 46, no. 2, 1999, pp. 146–85. JSTOR, http://www.jstor.org/stable/3270313. Accessed 21 Sep. 2022.

Bhabha, Homi K., 1949-. The Location of Culture. London; New York: Routledge, 2004. Krause, Julia. GRIN - the Deconstruction of Colonial Stereotypes in Contemporary English Fiction. 9 Dec. 2009, www.grin.com/document/141698.

Sebastian, By Meryl. "Netflix: Where Are the Indians Bridgerton Dreamed up Really From?"

BBC News, 9 Apr. 2022, www.bbc.com/news/world-Asia-India-61022232.

De, Anushka. "'Bridgerton' Is Another Disappointment in Indian Representation." Best of SNO, bestofsno.com/56318/arts-entertainment/bridgerton-is-another disappointment- in-Indian-representation. Accessed 30 Sept. 2022.

Van Eeden, Jeanne. "The Colonial Gaze: Imperialism, Myths, and South African Popular Culture." Design Issues, vol. 20, no. 2, 2004, pp. 18–33. JSTOR, http://www.jstor.org/stable/1512077. Accessed 18 Sep. 2022.

"Bridgerton Season2." NETFLIX, uploaded by Chris Van Dusen, Shondaland, 22 Mar. 2022, www.netflix.com.

Ramasubrhmanian, Srividya. "A Content Analysis of the Portrayal of India in Films Produced in the West." Core ac.uk, core.ac.uk/download/pdf/323308486.pdf. Accessed 22 Sept. 2022.

BIO-NOTE

Ameya Mary Yovakim serves as an Assistant Professor of English at St. Aloysius College, Edathua. Her research interests include Film Studies, Gender Studies, Post Modernism, and Cultural Studies.

CHAPTER VII

THE EMPOWERMENT OF WOMEN THROUGH SITA IN AMISH TRIPATHI'S SITA: WARRIOR OF MITHILA

Pattam Chakma

Ph. D. Research Scholar, Department of English

Dr. N. G. P. Arts and Science College

Coimbatore, Tamilnadu

ABSTRACT

Literature is a means to express life. The world is explored and expressed in various ways. Many writers write to express their viewpoint from their own perspective in order to enlighten the people. In a male dominated era, one of the most influential topics to discuss is the importance of women empowerment. One can observe the role of women in a society and how they are endowed and deprived of certain rights as compared to that of men. In the novel, *Sita: Warrior of Mithila*, Amish Tripathi highlights that the women are as capable as men are. They are powerful and can achieve any goal in their lives. Through his protagonist Sita, Amish compares and contrasts that women are as adequate as men mentally, socially, spiritually, physically and so on. Sita, the protagonist of the novel, is a notion of a role model for every woman in the society. This paper tries to conduct an honest review of the novel *Sita: Warrior of Mithila*, through its most powerful character Sita.

Key Words: Literature, life, women empowerment, warrior and role model.

The Empowerment of Women through Sita in Amish Tripathi's *Sita: Warrior of Mithila*

•••

In a country like India, women are still not independent of certain rights and occasions. Even though they are given equal opportunity like that of men, a woman still cannot go outside her house without the consent of her male companions. Sometimes, they are eve teased, thrown comments at and even brutally raped and killed. Every now and then, there is always news in the national television about women being molested, raped and even murdered. Recently in our country, on 25th September 2022, Ankita Bhandari's dead body was recovered from Chilla canal. Ankita, a nineteen-year-old receptionist is killed by her employer Pulkit Arya because she had denied sexual demand. In India, Hindu goddesses like Sita, Lakshmi, Kali, Durga, Ganga, etc. are worshipped all over, but the violence against women is a never-ending evil. Women are equally as blessed as men, except that they are physically weaker as compared to the opposite sex. Amish rightly states, "Women can be talented and competitive in the fields of knowledge, trading and labour. But when it comes to violence, the almighty has not blessed them with a natural advantage" (278).

Though so much has changed in the current society about the safety of the women, yet there is much to improve. The harassment of women is still a stigma in society. The government of India has taken different initiatives towards the advancement and safety of women. From the life of Amish's female protagonists, one can understand that when women are given a fair chance, they excel in every field. In the modern world, women have achieved the same as men in various fields like science, medicine, engineering, law, military, politics, education, etc. The novelist has portrayed his female characters from the highest rank as that of men who surpass in their own respective fields.

In the novel *Sita: Warrior of Mithila*, Amish portrays Sita as a powerful woman who is not only the ruler of a kingdom but also a great skilled warrior. She is kind, brave and fights against the injustice bestowed upon her. The novelist portrays Sita not only as a woman with capability but also as a role model to every single woman in the society. With her charisma and beauty, she impresses one of the finest men on earth, her husband Ram who finds beauty in character rather than out appearance. Amish tells, "Greatness usually comes at the cost of enormous suffering", Sita that has suffered is what makes her a great personality (181).

She is abandoned right after her birth. It is her good fate that Sunaina, the queen of Mithila found her in the jungle and adopted her as her own. At a very young age, she is sent to gurukul for education. Though Sita is a brave girl, she is terrified of leaving home. She loves her parents and often misses them. Sometimes, she has to face her fellow students who bullies her for being adopted. Sita is only fifteen years old when her mother passed away and being elected as the prime minister of Mithila, all the administrative responsibilities are upon her. But she excels in her duty. In praising her student, guru Shvetaketu says that "'She has the wisdom of King Janak...she also has the pragmatism and fighting spirit of Queen Sunaina" (51). This implies that Sita is not only an intelligent student but also a very skilled warrior. She is kind and an honourable person. In the novel, one can observe that there are people with deformities who are called Nagas. Many ostracised the Nagas but not Sita. Sita bonds with Hanuman, one of the Nagas. The duo is like the two siblings from the same parents who love and look after each other. Sita also holds a strong relationship with Jatayu, a Naga who respects and trusts Sita as the Vishnu. In the end of the novel, their strong bonding brings downfall to both of them while protecting one another.

Amish says that "A leader is not just one who leads. He must also be a role model (260). Sita's great deeds compels Vishwamitra to choose her as the Vishnu, a title given to the greatest leaders who are basically the Propagators of Good. Sita qualifies to be the Vishnu as she is a skilful warrior, intelligent, dedicated and hard working. Rosheena Zehra speaks of Sita in Thequint.com as "With this book, Amish has given us a Sita who is fielding armies single- handedly, is a champion archer, an efficient queen, and an able administrator. Additionally, it is refreshing to find a female protagonist in mainstream art whose physical appearance is not prioritised in her portrayal" (The Times of India). She and Vishwamitra discuss the plight of India and how they can overcome the various problems that are going on in and around India. One among many is the issue of the unfair birth-based caste system. In the olden days, a person's caste was based on his attributes, deeds and qualities. But that concept became corrupted as parents began to ensure their children remained in the same caste as them. Sita who represents good sees the injustice of the caste system and wishes to abolish it.

In the novel, other female characters like Sunaina, Samichi, Radhika and Manthara are well portrayed by the novelist who possesses power, courage and dignity in their respective positions. All these women represent something towards every woman and the society. Sunaina is portrayed as one of the strongest women of the novel. Being the queen of Mithila, she undertakes all the responsibilities of the kingdom while her husband dwells in the philosophy of knowledge. When she discovers Sita in the wood, she decides to adopt her as her own. She is kind and never distinguishes between her two daughters – Sita and Urmila. Her characteristics represent that every woman should fight for their own rights. Samichi is also a strong female figure. Even though she is a spy of Raavan, her role in Mithila as the police and protocol chief encourages many young women that a job in the military is as fascinating as any other job.

There is respect and honour being in the police force. On the other hand, Radhika is a representation of happiness. She stands as a symbol of peace and joy. Though she is in deep love with Bharath, the prince of Ayodhya, she breaks up with him because she seeks happiness in simple matters. She knows that Bharath loves her but what is most important for her is dwelling in that simple love with no royal duty and sacrifice like that of Bharath who has a larger duty towards his nation. She tells, "'It would be even worse if I married him and all my hopes for happiness were tied to nagging him to give up his dreams for India and for himself. I'd eventually make him unhappy. I'd make myself unhappy as well'"

(182). Through Radhika one can learn that happiness is not an accident but a choice that one can always make to be happy. Much like the other female protagonists, Manthara is portrayed as the richest merchant all over India. Her role indicates that hard work can make any one successful, whether man or woman, even if physically challenged just like her.

Sita, the propagator of good must not only be the role model to her people, but she must also practice and exercise her role as the Vishnu. Amish says, "I have portrayed her as a warrior, a strong woman. Strength here doesn't necessarily mean physical strength. It means being mentally strong as well, to have the ability to stand up and face challenges. Sita, in this book, has feminine power" (The Times of India). When Sulochan plans to kill her, she needs to stop him from harming her. According to Arishtenemi, a Vishnu unable to fight for oneself is incapable of fighting for others. Therefore, Sita hires Mara to kill Sulochan and who does succeed. As the novelist tells that "There is good and bad in everyone'", Sita's plot to murder Sulochan is not wrong (36). Sita is duty-bound to protect not only her family, but also her entire kingdom. In order to protect her loved ones, she must first protect herself. Her intention to defend from her enemies also indicates that one must fight to protect oneself from harm. One must protect and stand up against bullies.

Through Radhika one can also learn that personal happiness is as important as the happiness of others. Radhika decides to part ways with Bharath as soon as she realizes that she wouldn't be happy with him. Radhika stands up for her personal happiness. She knows that she couldn't be happy with Bharath marrying her because Bharath is a personality with larger cause towards his nation. While Radhika is a simple girl with less ambition and seeks happiness in simple things. Radhika choosing her personal happiness implies that one can always have the choice of being happy and normal. Radhika has the choice of choosing Bharath and living a luxurious life. But her happiness lies in being normal. She speaks, "I don't want to sacrifice anything. I just want to be happy. I just want to be normal'" (181). From the perspective of Sita and

Radhika, one must learn to stand up against any kind of injustice for personal safety and contentment. Therefore, women must fight for their equal share of rights, duties and honour.

CONCLUSION

In the current world, equal social set-up is less when compared to ancient India. In the olden days, women were equally respected and treated equally as men were. They hold positions of power and fought for their countries. Amish, through his novel, projects the importance of women and their role in society. Sita is not only a woman of talent but a fearless warrior. She fights with a lathi single-handedly with many combats and yet defeats them. Through Sati, the novelist inspires many women who can be equally strong as men are, mentally and physically. In order to highlight the importance of women empowerment, Amish mentioned a tribe called the Valmikis who are matrilineal. Their women do not marry outside their community. The Valmikis represent the existing matrilineal tribes of Meghalaya - Khasi, Jaintia and Garo tribes. In the novel, *Will You Still Love Me?* by Ravinder Singh, the protagonist, Lavanya speaks of the matrilineal tribe, "'Meghalaya is a state where the matrilineal structure is prevalent... 'It's the groom who has to live with the bride's family here and not the other way around. There's no dowry system here. Children inherit the mother's surname" (167).

WORKS CITED

Tripathi, Amish. Sita: Warrior of Mithila. Chennai: Westland Ltd, 2017.

The Times of India. Retrieved 3 April 2017.

Singh, Ravinder. Will You Still Love Me?. Gurgaon: Penguin Random House Pvt. Ltd, 2018.

Wikipedia contributors. "List of Hindu deities." Wikipedia, The Free Encyclopedia, 29 Sep.

2022. Web. 29 Sep. 2022.

Wikipedia contributors. "Sita: Warrior of Mithila." Wikipedia, The Free Encyclopedia, 1 Sep.

2022. Web. 30 Sep. 2022.

BIO-NOTE

Pattam Chakma is currently pursuing Ph. D. from Dr. N. G. P. Arts and Science College (Autonomous), Coimbatore under the Department of English. Before joining for Full-Time Ph. D., he worked as a school teacher for two years and as an Assistant Professor for one year in a college. Apart from teaching English as a subject, he also handled English Spoken classes. He studied B. A. English Literature from North Eastern Hill University, Shillong and M. A. English Language & Literature from Bharathiar University, Coimbatore. He specialises in writing morality, preservation and protection of the natural world, Good and Evil, etc. He has presented and published a number of papers in different journals in national and international platforms on various areas like Gender Studies, LGBT Rights, Nature and Human Values, etc.

CHAPTER VIII

FREAKS WITH IDENTITY: THE FEMALE DISABLED IN KATHERINE DUNN'S GEEK LOVE

Gayathry Pradeep M. A, M. Phil., B. Ed.

ABSTRACT

Impairment and disability are two confusing terms that appear when it comes to defining disability. Any psychological, physiological or anatomical structure or function of the body which is defective is termed impairment. The impact of impairment upon the performance of an individual is termed disability. There is a close relation between feminist and disability discourses as both tries to challenge the existing unequal social relations. Both fights against the concept of considering a category as deviant because of bodily features. The Portland born American novelist Katherine Dunn, and her novel Geek Love is of paramount importance in discussions regarding disability and feminism. The paper entitled, Freaks with identity: The female disabled in Katherine Dunn's *Geek Love* analyses how the author mocks the ableist notion of normalcy by portraying disabled women as central characters in her novel and thereby defining disability as an identity.

Key words: Disabled, Women, Binewski, and Identity.

Freaks with Identity: The Female Disabled in Katherine Dunn's *Geek Love*

• • •

Disability can be defined as a condition that restricts a person's everyday activities. It can be an impairment either intellectual, psychiatric, cognitive, neurological, sensory, physical or a combination of these. In some cases, it is permanent and is likely to be permanent in some other cases. Some disabilities are chronic and others episodic. A disability results in the reduced capacity of a person for communication, social interaction, learning or mobility and demands continuous support service.

It is a fact that people with disabilities, both men and women, are subjected to discrimination because of their disabilities. A comparative analysis reveals that disabled women suffer more segregation based on gender and based on disability. Traditional roles of women include the slots as nurturers, mothers, wives, and lovers. Women with disabilities fail to do these roles effectively which leads to their social ostracism.

Disability studies have adopted a gender blind approach to analyse the lives of people with disabilities. It has not yet recognized to the fullest sense the combined discrimination suffered by women with disabilities. It has not yet attained the standard to accommodate the needs of disabled women. The Disability Rights Act also neglected women from its primary concern. Just like almost all other movements, the focus of Disability movement too was on the male community. It is troubling to note that women with disabilities are being avoided by feminists as well.

Indeed, the Feminist Movement seems to have ignored the problems of women with disabilities. Even though feminist scholarship incorporated diverse experiences of women from various race, class, and other social, economic dimensions, women with disability were still excluded from their concern. Feminist writings of the body tend to focus on sexuality, pregnancy, monthly cycles, and mothering. The aspect of suffering, frustration, and torment was overlooked by feminists. As a result, women with disabilities feel that feminists have an ideal image of the female body and their bodies do not fit into these ideals. Their experiences cannot be included in the experiences of the female body. Thus the disabled female becomes a subaltern of sorts.

The double minority status experienced by women with disabilities, the lack of information about their lives, the need to change the situations leading to inequality of women, all these issues were discussed in detail in the book *Women and Disability: The Double Handicap* by M. J. Deegan and N.A. Brooks in the year 1985. It was an influential work. *Disabled, Female and Proud! Stories of 10 Women with Disabilities* is a 1988 book edited by Harilyn Rousso. The book provides positive role models for women and girls with disabilities. Featuring ten contemporary women with disabilities and their success stories, the book is an inspiration to many women with disabilities. As a result of the inspiration attained from these works, literary works began to be produced centering on the theme of disability.

Most of the works on disability written by women with disabilities very clearly portrayed the isolation, bitterness, despair, and marginalization faced by them. Other texts featuring disability were the exact opposite of this. They celebrated the achievement, happiness, and successes despite their struggles. There were also writings about disability from writers who are not disabled. Those works were written after a thorough study of the predicament of women with disabilities as the texts conveyed the social, economic and psychological circumstances of women with disabilities.

Mentally challenged women and women with developmental disabilities have been neglected by those theoreticians who have examined the employment situation of women with disabilities. The developmental disability field has recently devoted increasing attention to the importance of employment and a new federal initiative namely supported employment, has been developed with an aim to assist those with the most severe disabilities to get and hold a job. The newly found emphasis on employment in the field of developmental disabilities acknowledges the importance of productive work as a means to achieve social equality and financial independence, and supported employment programs are now being developed across the country.

The feelings of sympathy, fear or distaste are usually held by able bodied persons towards the disabled. In most cases people with disablity are portrayed as evil monsters, helpless and cruel. Segregation, forced sterilization were the inhuman practices by the able bodied in the name of racial purity. American history has a rich story to tell in terms of these evil practices.

The term 'grotesque' refers to a very ugly or comically distorted figure or image. It comes from the term 'grotto' referring to an underground place of burial or secrecy. They argue that menstruation, gestation, lactation adds to the grotesque feature of the female body. The disabled bodies were considered as grotesque by writers for a long period in literary history.

It is a custom that disabled women are more likely to be 'othered' than disabled men. Females in literary representation are subjected to objectification. It is a fact that very few authors include disabled females in novels as they are not praised by the readers.

In the contemporary United States, the condition is fast changing. Physical access to public sites and technology have all improved. This in turn made people participate in society and decision-making. Since the 1940s those who seek disability rights were active, but the rights became effective in the 1960s. Towards the latter part of the 20th century and early 21st century, there has been a movement towards acknowledging the normalcy of disability. This movement was evident in literature as well. It revealed its presence through the portrayal of disabled as evil and monsters to two dimensional presentations.

Katherine Dunn, a Portland born American novelist and voice artist, has written the novel titled *Geek Love* which is of paramount importance in the discussion of postmodern fiction featuring geeks. It was a revolutionary book in such a setting since it caricatured the Binewski family, a family that runs their own travelling freak show exhibiting their own freak children. The novel is unveiled through the perspective of Olympia, third child to the Binewski couple. Olympia is an albino, hunchbacked dwarf. Most of the characters in the novel are women and are disabled. The three women representing three generations of the Binewski family controls the plot of the novel. Olympia is seen compiling archives of their lives in the Fabulon in her own writings intended to be passed on to her daughter Miranda.

The women characters are not presented as introverts wailing at their condition of being disabled but as strong women who are proud of their specialty and unique identity. The Binewski Fabulon through the point of view of Olympia is vibrant and lively. She represents her family of women who assert themselves as extraordinarily talented and special. All together there are six major female characters in the novel including Crystal Lil, mother to the Binewski children, and wife of Aloysius Binewski; Olympia, the narrator of *Geek Love*; Miranda, daughter of Arturo and Olympia; Iphigenia and Electra, Siamese children born to the family of Fabulon. The girl with long pubic hair is the other female character in the novel appearing in the Glass House incident.

The narrator Olympia is a woman who has suffered patriarchal domination and succumbed to such a power in the early years of her life. The progress that she has achieved during the years till the present day when the novel happens shows the empowering of herself over the years. She was born to a family of geeks, where the father and mother are waiting for crippled children to develop their Fabulon. Olympia's special feature of having a hump and dwarfism was evident only on her third birthday. Till that time, she was not considered worthy by the parents to suit the business. Though her disability is evident, she was dismissed as irrelevant and not suitable, for she was not 'freak enough' for the business. This situation is ironic since Olympia was discriminated against in the family as a non-freak, whereas in society she was dismissed as a freak. The narrative describes the marginalization she suffered in her childhood days. The description of her performance at the Glasshouse and the audience's reaction asserts her transformation at such a level that she has the potential to mesmerize a crowd with her bodily features alone.

I am proud with my arrow tits flapping towards my knees, and the fat lady standing on my coat is staring, with spittle across her cheek, and the fat man with his electric G string pumping at his invisible crotch and laughing and the shouts coming up, "Christ! It's real!" The twisting of my hump feels good against the warm air and the sweat of my bald head runs down into my bald eyes and stings with brightness and the spirit of the waggling hump moves over the stage . . . While I stamp on my buttonless blouse, slide on the tangled elastic harness and open my near blind eyes wide so they can see that there is true pink there - the raw albino eye in the lashless-sockets- and it is good. (Dunn 28)

How conscious Olympia is about her body and identity is understood through her reaction when she sits as a model for Miranda to draw her picture. Olympia is enraged when she feels that Miranda does not respect her identity and that she gets reduced to a model in front of Miranda.

Thus, as the novel progresses, Olympia, the hunchbacked dwarf of a woman, instead of being doubly marginalized is seen emerging as a strong character. She is the mouthpiece of the writer. Olympia is the strong centre around which the plot revolves. She is the only character who knows that the other two Binewski women are living under the same roof as hers without acknowledging each other.

The other strong, rather the strongest, female character in the novel is the Binewski mother, Crystal Lil. The boarding house of Crystal Lil is the primary setting of the novel where Olympia, Miranda, and many other women live. At present she is seen as the in-charge of a ladies' hostel; she is also physically deformed. From the descriptions, she is deaf and partially blind. Her walking is also defective due to her poor eyesight.

Olympia says that Crystal Lil's eyesight is poor, that she grabs each vertical shape including humans on her way to support herself. It is said that "when someone takes offense, snaps or swears or pushes her away, she reels only momentarily before the next body presents itself and she hurtles on, using body after body as handholds through the air" (18). Crys' current situation of being deformed and fragile has a history to tell. Crystal Binewski, wife to Aloysius Binewski, was a mesmerizing Circus geek performer. She, along with her husband, took a strange decision to produce their own freak children for the family circus. She had consumed chemical drugs, isotopes and amphetamines during her pregnancy stage. It is the side effect of all those drugs that make her the way she is now.

In spite of having physical limitations, she is not shrunken to her household. Lil even in her late fifties is seen energetic and is running a hostel with a number of inmates including her own daughter and grandchild. She is portrayed as an adamant lady, strict to the inhabitants of the hostel. She gets irritated at times as well. Olympia points to an instance "Jingle of keys. High pitched burbling in the hall. Lillian delivering the mail. She is supposed to leave it on the table in the downstairs hall. Or, at most slit it under the doors. Sometimes she uses it as an excuse to come into the rooms" (20).

In Crystal Lil we see a strong woman. Instead of suffering double marginalization, being a woman and having disabilities, she represents a woman who is strong and capable of managing things on her own and also responsible for running a boarding house with more than thirty inmates. Lil is a strong woman that it is her ability that produced all the Binewski children as freaks so that the family could renew the business and become economically stable. Crystal Lil is the strong lady behind the success of the family show. Her identity as a woman and circus geek performer is clearly explained by the writer in the first session of the novel itself. Aloysius praises her for her acts in the Fabulon and her willingness to consume chemicals during the pregnancy stage and make her children amputated is indeed striking.

Aloysius details her daily routine of consuming the pills and cleaning the jars in which the exhibits are kept. The pill refers to the radioisotopes and chemicals that she consumes in her pregnancy stage to make her children disabled. Here we see a Lil who is profit-minded, a strong business lady indeed who is ready to create her own freak children. The cleaning of jars points to her affection as a mother. She cleans the jars where the aborted children, who couldn't survive the chemicals are kept. Lil considers these exhibits too as her children, and Lil's act of cleaning it daily by herself shows the love she has as a mother even to her aborted children.

The next female character introduced in the novel is Miranda. She is the daughter of Arturo and Olympia born not out of sexual intercourse, but by transferring Arturo's sperm to Olympia's ovary using the telekinetic powers of Fortunato. In those lines where Olympia remembers the first time she sees Miranda, we see a mother who is worried about her daughter born with only a minute deformation. The mother expected a child just like her father with pronounced disabled features.

Miranda is now a student at the Art Institute who is self-reliant, competent, hardworking and sincere in her studies. She appears to the world as a normal being since her tail is not evident at first sight. Her confusion about whether she should remove her tail, or maintain it is also discussed; but evidently, from the decision she makes, it is clear that she cannot easily be manipulated. Inspite of the rewards Ms. Lick offers her, Miranda stands in her firm decision to not remove her tail, accepts and asserts her identity.

Electra and Iphigenia are other women characters in the novel, both created by yet another experimental pregnancy of Crystal Lil. They were hailed as the magnificent musical Siamese twins "Elly and Iphy with their long hair smoothed into black buns, slim white arms entwined, pale faces beaming out in shafts from their violet eyes" (59). Their special features are described by Olympia as follows:

The girls were Siamese twins with perfect upper bodies joined at the waist and sharing one set of hips and legs. They usually sat and walked and slept with their long arms around each other. They were, however, able to face directly forward by allowing the shoulder of one to overlap the other. They studied the piano and began performing piano duets at an early age. Their compositions for four hands were thought by some to have revolutionized the twelve-tone-scale. (10)

From Olympia's description the reader gets an idea of Elly and Iphy as strong women protesting against the patriarchal attitude of their elder brother Arty. When Olympia in her early childhood longed for Arty's affection, and kept him as the role model, Iphy and Elly were brilliant enough to understand the authoritative mindset of Arty and resisted his control. They were always in a conflicting relation.

The decision to become sex workers was a revolutionary one on the part of the twins. It was a blow to the family patriarch Arty since the decision was against his wish. Elly and Arty converse that most of the guys are interested in their postures in bed, they are interested to fuck the twins. They are seen deciding to exploit that curiosity. This can be read in connection with the pro-sex war of the feminist wars of the 1970s and 80s. The pro-sex feminism emerged in the early 1980s which came about as a response to the anti-pornography movement in feminism. The proponents of the movement considered sexual freedom as of utmost importance in the fight for equality. They argued that sexuality is characterised by pleasure, not merely by intimacy and bonding. They considered obscenity laws and measures as restrictive to sexual expression.

Elly and Iphy's decision to become sex workers can be read in connection with this. Though the twin sisters were raped by the bagman several times with the support of Arty, and Elly was lobotomized with the help of Chick, the life they led was one of dignity and self-worth. They were never seen as bending to the authority of Arty. They always had a voice of their own and stood as strong women. The Twins' capability of altering the concept of family is evident when they give birth to their son Mumpo. This incident adds to the affirmation of sexuality by the twins. Instead of hiding on account of the shame of being raped, they give birth to the child as a revenge to the patriarchal Arty.

Another character who creates an identity with her physical feature is Denise, the girl with long pubic hair, who performs at the glass house. Denise is portrayed as such a strong lady who is able to live with her own choices about life. At one point she had decided to live with her disabilities and made monetary benefits. At another, she feels like removing her disability and she does it. She is also a strong woman in all phases of her life, both as disabled and normal. Towards the end of the novel, Olympia and Crystal Lil are the only two who survive the conflagration in the Fabulon. This can symbolically be read as a representation of the strength the women had to endure at any circumstance.

This novel featuring many disabled female characters is a saga presenting many strong women, who instead of being doubly marginalized, emerge as the empowered women from the Binewski Fabulon. Disability in the Fabulon is not something to be overcomed, but something to obtain. In a society where able bodies are hierarchically privileged, disabled subjects are expected to want to achieve able bodiedness to gain acceptance. Dunn mocks this ableist notion with crip grotesque humor, highlighting the absurdity of overcoming our specialties. By portraying disabled women as central characters, Dunn has adopted a new interpretation to the condition of being women and being disabled.

Dunn portrays each of her female characters as strong and capable. The women are independent and none is seen worried about the disabilities at any stage of the plot. The women are new faces of empowered women despite being disabled. For them, their unusual bodily feature is a source of their income. Each character is seen upholding his/her unique identity and is not enslaved to any source of power or authority.

The Postmodern novel featuring the geeks, exploring the freakish nature of characters from the perspective of the grotesque figure itself is indeed a new narrative trend. By inverting the hegemony of normal and abnormal, Katherine Dunn defines disability as a strong identity.

WORKS CITED

Deegan, Mary Jo, and Nancy A. Brooks, editors. *Women and Disability: The Double Handicap.*

Transaction Books, 1985.

Duffy, Yvonne. *All Things Are Possible.* A.J. Garvin and Associates, 1981.

Dunn, Katherine. *Geek Love.* Abacus, 2015.

Fine, Michelle, and Adrienne Asch. *Women with Disabilities: Essays in Psychology, Culture,* *and Politics.*Temple UP, 1988.

Hess, Abigail. *Katherine Dunn's Geek Love and the Question of Being Human in Freak Form.* 2017.

Rousso, Harilyn., editor. *Disabled, Female and Proud! Stories of 10 Women with Disabilities.*

Exceptional Parent Press, 1988.

Thomson, Rosemarie Garland. *Extraordinary Bodies: Figuring Physical Disability in American Culture and Literature.* Columbia UP, 1997.

Wendell, Susan. *The Rejected Body: Feminist Philosophical Reflections on Disability.* Routledge, 1996.

BIO-NOTE

Gayathry Pradeep, currently working as an English Teacher at Jyothi Public School Paika, Kottayam has completed her B. Ed. in English. She holds an M. Phil. Degree in English Language and Literature from Sree Sankaracharya University of Sanskrit, Kalady in the year 2020. Her postgraduation was at CMS College, Kottayam. She has cleared the UGC NET Examination in English and has one-year teaching experience as an English faculty at the Department of English, ICMS International College Manarcad, Kottayam. She has many paper presentations both in national and international seminars to her credit. Her area of research interest is Disability Studies.

CHAPTER IX

FEMININE SENSITIVITY AND PSYCHOLOGICAL CONFLICT IN ANITA DESAI'S WHERE SHALL WE GO THIS SUMMER?

Adarsh J. M. A., B. Ed.

ABSTRACT

The novelist such as Anita Desai, Arun Joshi and Jhumpa Lahiri delineate psychological conflict in their fictions. The protagonists of Desai often come in clash with the outside life, with others at individual level or with the society at large. With the passage of time and experience their mental perspective changes and it produces a psychic strain in them. The novel Where Shall We Go This Sumer? is replete with the instances of psychological conflict.

The paper entitled Feminine Sensitivity and Psychological Conflict in Anita Desai's *Where Shall We Go This Summer?* attempts to analyse Anita Desai's famous novel to find out the instances of feminine sensitivity in the life of Sita, the female protagonist, focusing on the Socio- cultural atmosphere of the metropolitan life and Sita's family atmosphere. The purpose of this paper is to note the marital disharmony in the life of Sita and her husband Raman. The main focus of this paper is to show how feminine sensitivity, marital disharmony, family relations and socio-cultural atmosphere are responsible for creating the feeling of loneliness in Sita and compelling her to alienate herself from family and society. Finally, to mark how Sita becomes the victim of psychological conflict and leaves the metropolitan city for an island.

Keywords: Conflict, feminine sensitivity, Sita, marital disharmony

Feminine Sensitivity and Psychological Conflict in Anita Desai's *Where Shall We Go This Summer?*

• • •

Anita Desai is a dominant figure in the twentieth century Indo Anglican fiction. One of India's best-known writers, Anita Desai has been among the voices that define the post- independence literary scene in India – not just as a writer, but also a chronicler of events that shaped the nascent republic though more often at a micro level than her contemporaries. She deserves accolades for her remarkable literary output. The relentless Anita Desai has brought out ten full-length novels of varied length, innumerable short stories and a couple of write-ups. In a short period of time, she has aroused a lot of critical attention; of late dozens of full-length critical assessments have been flooding the market.

Anita Desai is a bold and experimental novelist with a new sense and vibrant richness. Much attention is given to the emotional crisis of her protagonists who live in a chaotic society. Her famous novel *Where Shall We Go This Summer?* is a purely domestic novel which reveals the fluctuating emotional and mental states of the protagonist. It presents an internal drama of Sita's withdrawal from the stark realities of domestic life. The isolated life motivates the novelist to dissect the inner regions of human psyche. It is the purpose of this paper to critically analyse the theme of alienation in the novel *Where Shall We Go This Summer?*, and its title is based on this.

In novels where Anita Desai delineates a female protagonist, the struggle against the oppressive environment assumes the form of a patriarchal domination in one or the other visage, revealing her feminist predilections. She cares more for the individual in the comparison to the plot as pointed out by many critics, with an amazing insight into her psyche. The most significant social issue that Anita Desai focuses on is the institution of marriage-particularly in all the novels where women is the protagonist. When a woman is caught in the trap of marriage, she has one way left, which is to languish in misery. Each novel of Anita Desai is progressively a search of the self for a heightened female awareness.

She portrays and analyses human relationships in the context of emotionally related kin which is a fertile area for exploration. As J. P. Tripathy observes;

Desai possesses one of the healthiest and psychologically most balanced minds in the realm of Indo-Anglian fiction and the sanity of her tastes and attitudes, is almost exemplary, a point worth emulation for her fellow religionists in the field of writing. As a woman writer she does not profess to be a feminist and yet she voices the fears and concerns, the hopes and aspirations of her characters in her own artistic way. (Tripathy 1)

Feminine Sensitivity and Psychological Conflict

Anita Desai is interested in the psychic life of her characters and her novels reveal that her real concern is with the exploration of human psyche. Desai's main concern is to peel off layer after layer the human mind. She is interested in the psychic life of her characters. *Where Shall We Go This Summer?* brings forth the agonized self and feminine sensitivity of the protagonist, Sita.

Feminism is a world-wide cultural movement to secure a complete equality of women with men in the enjoyment of all human rights - moral, religious, social, political, educational, legal, and economic and so on. It means a sense of personal courage. The feminist consciousness or sensitivity is the consciousness of victimization. As a philosophy of life, it seeks to discover and change the more subtle and deep-seated causes of women's oppression. It opposes women's subordination to men in the family and society. It is a global and revolutionary ideology.

The study of Anita Desai's novels reveals that she wishes to project the psychological temperaments of the human mind. Psychological conflicts are innate and natural processes of the mind. The conflict occurs when individuals perceive their thoughts, views, attitudes, goals and interests contradicted by other individuals or social groups. In *Where Shall We Go this Summer?*, Desai delineates Sita's feminine sensitivity and the other factors leading the psychological conflict in her.

Sita lives in the metropolitan city, Bombay, with her husband Raman and her four children. She is pregnant for the fifth time. She is not happy in the present surrounding. She finds modern life full of violence and commotion. Moreover, her husband, Raman, does not pay attention to her feelings. Her children engage themselves in such activities, which are disliked by her. The incidents which upset her are – the fighting of cook and her ayah, ayahs quarreling on the streets, breaking of buds by Menaka, and tearing the paintings to strips and dropping them on the floor by Menaka. All these instances upset and frighten Sita. It stirs Sita's feminine sensitiveness. It leads the way for psychological conflict in her mind. She decides to leave Bombay and go to the island Manori to save her fifth child from the din and bustle of metropolitan life. She doesn't want to give birth to her child in such atmosphere. Noticing Sita's reaction to the surrounding incidents. Sita is estranged from her husband and children because of her emotional reactions to the incidents that occur to her in society.

The incident of eagle-crows fight in the novel reveals extreme feminine sensitiveness of Sita. From the balcony of her flat she sees that some crows are attacking on an eagle. The eagle is struggling to save himself from the attack of crows. Looking this scene, she decides to save the eagle from the attack of crows. She shouts for her sons and asks Karan to bring the toy gun. While fetching toy gun Karan falls down and his chin is cut; but Sita ignores it and she herself fetches the toy gun and shots it at crows. This shows how she is eager to save eagle. They reach to eagle to see whether it is dead or alive. The older boys declare it as dead. Next morning there is nothing on the ledge but some feathers and some stains of blood. It indicates that the eagle is eaten by the crows. Raman with his morning cup of tea says to her, "They've made a good job of your eagle." (Desai 37) She replies to him "perhaps it flew away." (Desai 37) But she is sure that it might not have flown away. Through this episode, the novelist wishes to reveal Sita's feminine sensitivity. This episode symbolizes Sita's conflict with her husband and her struggle for supremacy at a deeper psychological level. Here, eagle is the symbol of Sita and Rama is the symbol of crows that attack on the helpless eagle. Sita's desperate effort to save the eagle from the attack of the crows is her fight against the masculine values represented by her husband, Raman. On this eagle- crows fight episode Dr. M. Maini Meitei, aptly remarks:

'Sita's words "perhaps it flew away?" against her husband's caustic remark that her eagle has been eaten by the crows, suggests the future course of her action following her defeat and loss of identity. (.M.Maini Meitei 35-36)'

After this incident Sita's urge to leave Bombay and go to Manori increases. She hurriedly packs and leaves for Manori Island in complete defiance of her husband's hhypocritical world. She returns to her father's island, charmed by him. This is, indeed, her last effort to try to save her identity by showing her faith in her father's magic world. ostile and

The theme of marital disharmony is also noted in this novel. The marital life of Raman and Sita is not smooth. Almost all female protagonist of Anita Desai are the victims of marital disharmony. Desai has presented marital disharmonies as they exist in Indian male dominated traditional families. Desai's forte is her handling of maladjusted marriages. Maya (in *Cry the Peacock*), Monisha (in *Voices in the City*) and Sita (in *Where Shall we Go This Summer?*) are all women of deep emotions and fine sensitivities who are entrapped in marriages with men who are never out rightly cruel, who carry out their husbandly obligations assiduously but are impervious to their wives' pleas for understanding, communication and respect for their individuality. Such emotionally incomplete relationships have a fatal effect on the finely turned female psyche and Desai's women find themselves tortured by a painful sense of alienation.

In *Where Shall we Go This Summer?*, the marital disharmony results from the conflict between two irreconcilable temperaments and two diametrically opposed viewpoints of Sita and Raman. Sita notices that her husband pays too much attention to his business without caring her feelings. Sita finds her life dull and monotonous.

She anticipates Raman to be the life lover, making her realize how valuable she is to him. Raman however does not fulfill her wishes. Raman focuses his energies on his business and becomes an escapist. He has his own morals, and own standards. Consequently, the temperaments of Sita and her husband remain poles apart. Sita is quite disgusted with the friends and businessmen who come to meet Raman. She remarks about them: "They are nothing--nothing but appetite and sex. Only food, sex and money matter. Animals." (Desai 43) Sita observes that the people in Bombay are just for materialistic life. When Sita finds her life lack of love of Raman, she starts smoking. It indicates Sita's psychic balance is disturbed. Over Sita's behaviour Dr. M. Maini Metei remarks: "Sita is a hypersensitive, an introverted personality and a pessimist." (M. Mani Metei 31)

When Raman does not fulfill her wishes, Sita feels marital dissatisfaction with her husband. She is not happy with her present life. Sita's problem seems to be due to maladjustment with her husband, the home life and the surrounding atmosphere nauseating her. The root cause of marital discord between Sita and Raman lies in the fact that Raman marries Sita not out of love but "out of pity, out of lust, out of sudden will for adventure, and because it was inevitable married her." (Desai 89) After marriage Sita lives with Raman's family members for some days. But she feels uncomfortable with her in-laws. Noticing Sita's condition Raman comes to live in a small flat. But here too "people continued to come and be unacceptable to her." (Desai 45) She is fed up with her husband, a businessman, whose complete lack of feeling brings her to the verge of insanity. She spends almost all her time on the balcony, smoking, looking out at the sea. Sita notices that her husband ignores her instincts, and what she likes him to treat her in a gentle and tender way is what he cannot do. The people who come to visit Raman are his friends, visitors, business associates, colleagues or acquaintances. He regards them with little humor and with restraint. With some he does business, with others he eats a meal. Just for the sake of his friends, visitors and business associates he ignores the feelings of Sita. And that hurts Sita. Sita not only hates Raman for his lack of feeling but also derides the "subhuman placidity, calmness and sluggishness" (Desai 43) and the routine manner of her husband's family. As a reaction against these, when she speaks with rage and anguish, and with "sudden rushes of emotion, as though flinging darts at their smooth, unscarred faces" (44). This strange behavior of Sita is the exhibition of psychological conflict created in her mind. Over Raman's lack of feeling for Sita, Dr. M. Maini Meitei rightly remakes: "In the long-run the husband-wife relationship is dragged into difficulties that come out in the form of identity crisis, for both Raman and Sita stand for binary oppositions. (Meitei 31)

As Sita is disgusted with the strange and insensitive nature of Raman, she finds a kind of pleasure in the common scenes she happens to see. Firstly, the sight of a foreign tourist who wants to go to Ajanta without knowing which direction he has to go. Once, Raman and Sita are coming "back from a week's holiday exploring the Ajanta and Ellora caves." (Desai 45) Their car is stopped by a foreigner for the lift for going to Ajanta. Raman replies to the foreigner, "I' m sorry, we've just come from Ajanta we're going the other way." (Desai 46) The foreigner apologizes. Raman advises him gently—"If you want a lift to Ajanta, you had better cross the road and stand on that side." (Desai 46) This reveals that Raman is a kind and co-operative person. After this incident Sita thinks repeatedly of that foreigner. Raman asks her "why she had once more brought up the subject of the hitchhiking foreigner, months later." (Desai 47) Over this, Sita blurts out: "He seemed so brave," (47). To this, Raman replies: "Brave? Him? He was a fool _ he didn't even know which side of the road to wait on." (47) Sita replies quickly: "Perhaps that was only innocence, and it made him seem more brave not knowing anything but going on nevertheless." (47) Here, Sita wants to compare the foreigner with Raman and thinks that foreigner is braver than Raman. When Sita says that the foreigner is a brave man, Raman replies to her with annoyance in his voice, "you seem to admire him a lot. You would have liked to know him better, it seems." (47) To this, Sita replies instantly, "I would. I would like to travel that myself." (47) This discussion between Raman and Sita marks that they do not tolerate each-other's remarks very easily. And this creates a kind of rift between them. It leads their marital relationship towards disharmony. Furthermore, this incident also marks Sita's firm decision to go to island Manori, like the foreigner who travels without knowing anything about the place Ajanta. Second instance is noted when Raman comes to Manori island, to take Meneka back to Bombay. Sita complaints to Raman about her past life in Bombay and says to him: "Do you know in all these years. We've lived together, in Bombay, I have known only one happy moment?" (132). She narrates the incidents of Hanging Garden to Raman. One evening she took her children to the Hanging Garden. There she saw a young Muslim woman in the lap of an old man, an unworldly sight. She says:

They were like a work of art _ so apart from the rest of us. They were not like us - they were inhuman, divine. So strange _ that love, that sadness, not like anything I've seen or known. They were so white, so radiant, they made me see my own life like a shadow, absolutely flat, uncolored.

These words of Sita indicate that she desires the love from Raman, like that of Muslim woman and the old man. But she is heartbroken as she doesn't get that kind of love from Raman. All these incidents make her think that her identity is lost in this kind of atmosphere, where she finds no feeling in Raman's heart and the metropolitan life of Bombay, full of din and buzle. It shatters the husband - wife relation. And she packs her things and leaves for Manori, the magic island of her father. Here Sita alienates herself from the family members and the society. It is also an aspect of psychological conflict. After analyzing this novel, we can agree with the view of B. Chitra about the novels of Desai. She remarks:

The novels of Anita Desai catch the bewilderment of the individual psyche confronted with the overbearing socio- cultural environment and the ever- beckoning modern promise of self-gratification and self-fulfillment. (Chitra 216)

Thus, like the other protagonists of Desai's novels, Sita also becomes the victim of socio-cultural and family atmosphere and loses her psychic balance. The incidents such as fighting of cook with ayah, quarreling of ayahs on the streets, disturbances of children at home, Raman not paying any attention to her feelings and her problem to adjust with Raman's family members, lead the way for psychological conflict in her mind. And in the attack of psychological conflict, she desires for loneliness. She alienates herself from Raman and society and leaves for the island Manori with her daughter Menaka and son Karan.

If we delete summer from *Where Shall We Go This Summer?*, the perennial question remains- where shall we go? The confusion as is obtaining today is worse confounded; for the citadel of conscious and value had almost crumbled or is likely to crumble. The brute force of money, Corruption, machines, automations, scepticism and violence have resulted in despair, maladjustment, divorce, rape, illicit sex, melancholy and frequent emotional and psychological breakdowns. Nobody feels secure; even mothers feel scared giving birth to their children, not to talk of providing security to the children already wanting in nutrition and prosperity. Sita our protagonist is greatly confused not finding a fit society where she can breathe calmly and where she can give birth to her child. Desai has raised a question of crisis of conscience and values of universal importance in this novel.

Sita's wish in this novel to hold back the birth of her fifth child by magic is the product of her sick mind. With the paranoiac rage, enigmatic demands and querulous behavior Sita makes herself and her family miserable. The insane obstinacy of her wish to hold back to the child, and the overwhelming despair put her in the category of Desai's earlier protagonists heading for a neurosis, psychosis or sudden end. However, her final resolution to reconcile with life saves her from a melodramatic, drastic end. Sita shifts from compliance to rebellion and then to withdrawal, again coming back to compliance. Her unusual behavior coupled with the intense stress and trauma in her life make her complex character and this complexity adds to the tension of the plot.

A person cannot live in the imaginary world all the while. He/she must be mindful of reality. If Sita had remembered this truth of life, perhaps she won't have faced the mental agonies she faced in the novel. The novel presents the fact of Indian society before us. Being a woman, she may imply through the presentation of Raman Sita that man should be as ideal as Ram of the Ramayana and Sita as sacred as the mythological Sita. But this idealism of Desai in modern, materialistic world will, no doubt remains a dream. However, a sort of message she wanted to give is that one should be not imaginary like Sita forgetting the way of the world or should not be as practical as Raman, neglecting the basic need and feeling of his wife. Perhaps Desai expects Utopian world where every individual can live a peaceful and playful life. Through her depiction of Raman, she does not seem to blame him, neither does she seem to defend Sita for her whims. She presents them as life like characters. This is one of the major reasons why the novel appeals to us. The problems faced by the Sita, Raman and their children are not their problems alone, but the problems of all of us. And the way out for all of these problems is not to go to extremity but think over them silently and to enable ourselves and other to lead a peaceful life. She conveys the message of life through Sita that despite all calamities, anxiety, and frustration life is worth living.

The world of Anita Desai's novels is an ambivalent one, it is a world where the central harmony aspired to but not arrived at, and the desire to love and live clashes at times violently with the desire to withdraw and achieve harmony. In all her novels there is a striving, on the part of the protagonist towards arriving at a more authentic way of life than the one which is available to them. There is a need to be loved. The same is true in the case of Sita in *Where Shall We Go This Summer?*.

WORKS CITED

Chitra. B. "The Enigmatic Maya in Anita Desai's Cry, the Peacock", Language in India, Vol.

10, 2010. 216.

Desai, Anita. *Where Shall We Go This Summer?* Orient Paperbacks, 2008. Jain, N. R. A

Critical Study of thr Novels of Anita Desai. Atlantic, 1999.

Jain, Jasbir. Stairs to the Attic: The Novels of Anita Desai. Jaipur: Printwell, 1987.

Meitei, M. Mani. "Anita Desai's Where Shall We Go This Summer? A Psychoanalytical Study". Quest for Identity in Indian English Writing Part 1: Fiction. Ed. R. S. Prathak. Bahri, 1992. 30-42.

Prasad, Hariom. "Anita Desai's Where Shall We Go This Summer? as a critique of

existentialism".

Studies in Indian Writing in English. Ed. RajeshwarMittapalli. Atlantic, 2004. 112-119.

Prathak, R. S. "The Alienated Self in The Novels of Anita Desai".The Fiction of Anita Desai.

Ed. R. K. Dhawan. Bahri, 1989. 17-38.

Rani, Usha. Psychological Conflict in the Fiction of Anita Desai, Abhishek Publications,

2006. Rao, Ramachandra B. The Novels of Anita Desai. Ludhiana: Kalyani,1977.

Sidney, Finkelstein. Existentialism and Alienation in American Literature. International,

1965. Sridevi, M. "Theme of reconciliation in Anita Desai's Where Shall We Go This Summer?

A Study". The Indian Review of World Literature in English. Vol. 5. January, 2009.

Srivastava, Ramesh. K.Six Indian Novelist in English. Guru Nanak Dev University, 1987.

Swain, S, P. "The Dialectics of Marital Polarization in Anita Desai's Cry, the Peacock.

Studies in Indian Writing in English. Ed. Rajashwar Mittapalli. Atlantic, 2004. 95-111.

Tripathy,J. P. The Mind and the Art of Anita Desai. Bareilly: Prakash, 1986.

BIO-NOTE

Adarsh J., is currently working as an English teacher at Sri Vidyaniketan Public School, Sriram Nagar, Karnataka. He completed his B.Ed. in English from Titus II Teachers College, Thiruvalla. He holds an M.A Degree in English Language and Literature from CMS College, Kottayam in the year 2017. His Under Graduation was at Sree Narayana College, Kollam. He has cleared the KTET Examination in English and has one-year Teaching Experience as an English faculty at St Mary's Residential School, Pathanapuram. He also completed a Post Graduate Certificate Course for Personal Development from CREST, Calicut.

CHAPTER X

REITERATING PATRIARCHY THROUGH STEREOTYPING FAMILY ROLES IN ADVERTISEMENTS

Harsha Anna Kuriakose

MA English Language and Literature & MBA in Human Resources

Senior Customer Service Specialist.

ABSTRACT

New media and technology are influencing the society in many ways. The constant evolution makes it clear how huge its impact is on everyone. They are also involved in reiterating the existing patriarchal norms by means of stereotyping roles of men and women in every family. People often try to imitate advertisements. And more than considering the product's usefulness they tend to identify themselves with the people in the ads by using these products. And these ads have their vested interests and hidden agenda as well. A thorough and detailed analysis of the sign system used in the ads help us to understand these interests and agendas better. Since ads act as the medium between products and consumers and there is a great tendency to believe and imitate blindly whatever is shown in ads, a study to find out the hidden meanings of advertisements is relevant. This article outlines the origin and developments of ads across time, and tries to find how changes in the field of advertising effectively propagate or reinforce the patriarchy, precisely by stereotyping gender roles in family.

Keywords: Advertisements, patriarchy, reiteration, and Cultural theory.

Reiterating Patriarchy through Stereotyping Family Roles in Advertisements.

• • •

INTRODUCTION

Advertisements, the most popular and widely accessed media form in both print and electronic formats, have undergone radical transformations since inception. Being one of the most influential and powerful media or expressions in the modern world, these are used effectively in stimulating sales and purchases. Encyclopaedia Britannica defines advertisements as: the techniques used to bring products services, opinions, or causes to public notice for the purpose of persuading the public to respond in a certain way toward what is advertised. Most advertising involves promoting a good that is for sale.

Generally, advertisements are believed to create an interest or a kind of necessity in the buyers by making an acceptance for a product and thus mainly concerned with presenting the information about the product in such a way that it provokes the "buying moves of potential customers" (Fatihi, 2). These advertisements have undergone many turns and fluxes of time and have changed dramatically in terms of representations. This does not get limited to a supposedly realistic introduction of this item but getting adapted to a more believable atmosphere where they portray the product as inevitable and irreplaceable in an individual's day today life. Depicting a product in such a manner, it becomes an individual's status marker, question of prestige and thereby advertisements make one buy that product which in turn stands for a cluster of values and norms. The advertisements which function primarily as commercial tools are used to motivate or alter the buying behaviours the customers.

Moreover, advertisements also reduce the distance between consumers and goods and indirectly play a vital role in increasing consumption among consumers. Fatihi sums up such a situation accurately when he says "ads are a boon" if they are used "honestly". (Fatihi 2)

Apart from the role as a commercial tool, in the present times advertisements have become more like a cultural and social text.

Advertisements, whether in print media or electronic media, convey the intended message with the help of signs, which are made of both signifiers and signifieds. While, in the print media the meaning heavily depends on how one perceives it, in the electronic media a particular meaning is imposed on its viewers, as superior to all possible interpretations. More than advertising a product, they are now focusing on depicting how important this product is in every household and thereby create an urge in every individual to buy it. In that process, they start to incorporate these products, referred to as "objects" by Baudrillard, into the domestic situations (25). They twist the reality to create a world in which their product occupies the centre thereby showing that an individual cannot survive in this highly competitive world without their products. Entering into every realm of one's life, advertisements now have an irrefutable influence on individuals, irrespective of age and gender. More than assessing or valuing the usefulness of the product before them, people often want to imitate the people in the advertisements, with the belief that only such an imitation helps them to achieve a status, respect, value in the society as the characters in the advertisements.

Advertisements: A Historical Overview

The origin of advertisements can be traced back to ten thousand years ago. Outdoor display was the most commonly used method in the beginning which were more "passive" and extremely limited in their scope. Antecedent to this, the origin can be traced back to the three thousand years old papyrus sheets used in Egypt, announcing the reward for the return of run-away slaves and other decisions by government. There also existed "stenciled inscriptions" on bricks and also "town criers" who shouted out the things-to-be-noted. Printed advertisements played less role until the invention of the printing press by Johannes Gutenberg in 1445 post which produced in more quantities and distributed widely.

Broadly speaking the history and development of advertisements can be divided into six periods;

o Pre-printing period

o Early printing period

o Period of expansion

o Period of consolidation

o Period of scientific development

o Period of business and social integration

History and Development of Advertisements in India

Right from the early days of Indian civilization, one can find the uses of advertisements. Remnants of Harappa and Mohenjo-Daro indicate the stones and earthen plates on which names are engraved, which are more or less similar to the present-day trade mark system. In India the early forms of advertisements were chiefly used for religious purposes, which means, it was in the form of propaganda. The forerunners of advertisements can thus be traced back to the rocks and pillars, set up according to the orders of emperor Ashoka, in order to spread the teachings of the Buddha. Some others also hold the view that advertisements started with the "hawkers" calling out their wares right from the days when cities and markets first began.

It was only during and after the British rule that advertisements began to be used for business purposes in India as they needed advertisements to popularize their products, especially luxury goods. They also introduced the print media which helped in the origin and flourishing of newspapers. The origin of commercial advertisements in India is a recent phenomenon. It was only in the beginning of the 20th century that advertisements in print media attained a considerable significance. Many other factors also played their role well like educational development, popularization of media etc. Technological advancements like computer graphics have further influenced/changed the functioning of advertisements in India and brought a new power and identity to the production of advertisements in our country.

The Development of Advertisements in Kerala

Government notifications were the first form of advertisements existed in Kerala and this was brought to the notice of people by beating drums followed by the advertisements of medicines appeared in newspapers. Advertisements on medicines assumed a superior position among others in the print media during the first decades of 20th century. A notable change occurred towards the middle of 20th century when the publishers of newspapers canvassed the advertisers to give their advertisements on the front page. Advertisers in the 20th century started to structure/arrange their advertisements with the pictures of their products and its services along with catchy words and captions.

The emergence of Film Exhibitors in Kerala necessitated an increasing number of advertisements for films, in order to attract public to the cinema. The development in this field also witnessed film advertising which lasted for a short time span of 2 or 3 minutes and later on, it also became popular as well. Towards the last two decades of the 20th century, cosmetic items had attracted the women folk through the wide popularity of the advertisements in magazines especially in women magazines like Vanitha, Gruhalakshmi etc. The wide publicity led to the increased consumption of their products across the State. It was in 1982 that radio started to broadcast commercial ads and by 1985 Malayalam programs also appeared on TV. Both these factors played significant and dominant roles in popularizing advertisements. The wider geographic coverage of these electronic media contributed to the increasing publicity of advertisements among the people.

Slowly we have come to a situation where products as well as different institutions, establishments, etc., have their existence only through effective advertisements. It paved the way for competition among advertising agencies and even among media for their survival. In such a context, print and electronic media have started canvassing advertisers even without checking the genuineness and validity of these advertisements. Thus, some misleading, fake advertisements have also been seen during these times.

The twenty first century has witnessed a rapid advance and flourishing of advertisements. Starting with mere description or write ups of products, now advertisements have become more like a mini-movie that tempt every family and individual to buy the product they advertise. One can undeniably declare that advertisements have undergone a stupendous transformation across time and it is still getting adapted to the flux of the trends in the contemporary society.

Advertisements: A Theoretical Overview

Advertisements undoubtedly facilitate large scale marketing as it is a medium of mass communication. Now a days all companies are spending a huge sum of money on advertisements to carry the messages to "the intended public or consumers" through different media like tv, radio, internet, newspapers, magazines etc (Fatihi 17). It clearly points to the influence and popularity these advertisements have made among the people, that too in such a highly competitive and consumer-oriented marketing. The main purposes of advertising are to "give information, attract attention, create awareness, and influencing the buying behaviours of consumers". According to Gaurav Akrani, the term "advertising" comes from the Latin word "advertere" which means "to turn the mind towards". It is in fact a "marketing vehicle" to make people aware of the newly manufactured product.

Akrani also lists some of the features of advertisements in his rather elaborate blog. The primary purpose of advertising is to provide "appropriate information" about the products or services to the prospective buyers. This includes features of the product, uses, prices, benefits etc. Secondly it is a "paid communication" that aims at "the persuasion of potential customers". It greatly tempts the consumers to buy the product. These advertisements heavily influence the buying decisions of customers. Advertising becomes effective and fruitful only if they are target oriented. This means advertisements focus mainly on market and its consumers and not individuals. Advertisements are generally accepted as work of art as it has got a creative part, science as it has rules and principles to follow and a profession as well. It has largely got a creative part which is called the "essence of advertising". Akrani also points out the "Five Mo" that is to be taken care of while making decisions regarding the advertisement: Mission, Money, Message, Media and

Measurement.

AIDA is the acronym, used in marketing and advertising, for Attention, Interest, Desire and Action. Developed by E. St. Elmo Lewis in 1898, it is a model which is widely used, even today, to measure the effectiveness of every advertisement. According to this theory or model every advertisement needs to attract the attention of the people, generate an interest in the client, create enthusiasm in public, and make people buy these products. Another theory named Means-End theory discusses the motive of advertisements. According to this theory advertisements mostly contain a message that leads the customer to a desired goal.

The 20th century can be very well described as a "century of consumption" (Nayar 118). Jean Baudrillard in his book makes it clearer when he says that human beings are surrounded by the "fantastic conspicuousness of consumption and abundance" (25). This abundance is not that of human beings, but of "objects" (25). Globalisation, emergence of metropolitan cities etc. have changed the culture of consumption in people and indirectly it has affected the advertisement industry as well. Citing from Philip Kotler, Nayar presents the "four Ps" of consumption and marketing: the "Product", the "Placement of the product", the "Promotion of the product" and the "Price of the product" (126). The Four Ps are in "alignment" with the modes of selling, marketing, its rhetoric, etc (127).

Representation is very crucial in advertisements. A commodity is reduced to a sign when abstract qualities are represented as a product or object. The representational part is described as the "narrative part of advertisements" (Nayar 130). The advertisements, according to Nayar, "generate the desire for the product" in consumers and is "inextricably linked to the theme of lifestyle" (132). The rhetorics of advertisements tend to create a relationship or a kind of identification between the product and the consumers. Nayar makes it clear that the product is projected as a "component of an identity we desire" (135). Through advertisements the commodity is becoming a sign and advertisements are becoming linguistic and cultural texts carrying different meanings and implications.

Advertisements are intertwined with the creation of desired identities. First of all, advertisements present a situation that the consumer would like to be in. Even though it works at the fantastical level it incorporates the real needs and necessities of people into it. Mostly all advertisers create the consumers as "aesthetes" who can enjoy the beauty of objects (Nayar 134). Secondly, these advertisers try to incorporate the idea of national identity through the advertisements. For this they set the whole ad in a localised background and thus indigenization of identity is emphasized. Finally, the advertisers link the individual consumer to the group of other consumers who use this product and propose "a union of consumers, united in trust" (136). Thus, advertisements construct certain identities through representations and invariably link them to the advertised products or commodities. The prerequisite to identity formation is large scale consumption of goods.

Theodor Adorno and Max Hokheimer, two important philosophers of the twentieth century, in their essay titled "The Culture Industry: Enlightenment as Mass Deception" say that the upcoming media forms are trying to make up "a system which is uniform as a whole and in every part" (1). This "striking unity" has paved way for a kind of monopoly of the large scale industries. They have also noted the fact that "under monopoly all mass culture is identical" (1). The truth is highly ironical that it is these media themselves who "manipulate retroactive needs" and make the unity grow even stronger (Adorno and Hokheimer 1). These philosophers use the term "movies" in their discussion in which we can safely include present day's advertisements. According to them "real life is becoming indistinguishable" from all these (4). Individuals begin to imitate these models in the media in a greater extent which lead to blind reiteration of the existing systems. Every media presents a stylized mode and along with its presentation, occurs a "universal imposition" of the same (Adorno and

Hokheimer 5). And in advertisements too, which carry a storyline embedded within the family, this imposition of the existing systems is evident. In the era of culture industry what is absolute is "imitation" (Adorno and Hokheimer 6). With a believable, domestic atmosphere the audience who are customers also are forced to imitate or consume what is presented as "component of an identity we desire" (Nayar 133).

The "harmony" gets inaugurated by "craftily sanctioning the demand for the rubbish" (Adorno and Hokheimer 8). They further go on to state, "in view of the ideological truce, the conformism of the buyers and the effrontery of the producers who supply them prevail. The result is a constant reproduction of the same thing" (8). Similar to how this uniformity in demand leads to the manufacturing of the same goods, advertisements make a unity among customers who are supposed to follow the way things are presented before them. Thus, not only products are 're-produced', but the system or ideology in it also get reiterated. There are no individuals as such, having an identity of their own, rather they are "an illusion" according to Adorno and Hokheimer (18). Every individual is a part of the larger whole, whose ultimate identity, portrayal etc. are heavily determined by this multimedia even through advertisements.

The 20th Century philosopher Jean Baudrillard, in his book clearly states that advertising has a "strategic position" in the process of transforming "object into an event" (126). The strategy of advertisements "targets everyone in their relation to others, in their hankerings after reified social prestige" (Baudrillard 64). According to Baudrillard, the system "appropriates social objectives for its own gain, and imposes its own goals as social objectives" (72). Advertising, according to him, "as a whole has no meaning"; instead it conveys certain "significations" which carries the intended message (88). Thus, advertisements come with a "background function", to provide a "repetitious, reassuring backdrop of signs" (121). He also presents his view that, advertising is becoming more "homogenous" which is highly "subjected to the same labour of myth-making" (126). He even goes to the extent of saying that the "successful advertiser is the master of a new art", not because he presented it all new, rather as an art of "making things true by saying they are so" (127). By presenting it true, the audience blindly take what is presented in advertisements as a lifestyle to be followed, and there lies the success of an advertiser.

Raymond Williams, in one of his essays, "Advertising: the magic system", makes a detailed study of the advertisements and its development where he presents a new finding of his research that the place of advertisements in contemporary society goes much far beyond its commercial purposes. Especially in the past decade, advertisements had "passed the frontier of the selling of goods and services and has become involved with the teaching of social and personal values" (Williams 334). In the editor's introduction, he calls advertisements "magic" as "it transforms commodities into glamorous signifiers", which again takes us to Nayar's opinion of advertisements as presenting every commodity as a component of one's desired identity.

In most of the contemporary advertisements, the existing patriarchal system is reinforced, through the 'underrepresentation" of women in media, according to the findings of Julia T Wood (1). According to her, women are "underrepresented" which in turn reinforces "men as the cultural standard" and "women as invisible" (1). In fact, the "underrepresentation" of women distorts the actual reality and moulds different truth favourable to some section of the population (Wood 1).

With many noteworthy developments in the field of advertisements, they have taken a great leap from a mere presentation of the product to an acceptable portrayal of the same in a more domestic situation. The complex structuring of advertisements focuses not only on advertising the product but on the importance of family as well. In most of the advertisements, we can see a stereotyping of the family roles, which reiterates patriarchal norms and restrict the movement of women to the outside world from the confining domestic circle. Some select advertisements are analysed using all these different perspectives and an attempt is made to find out how stereotyping is done to limit women even in a much developed and developing societies.

Critical Analysis of Select Advertisements

Caught up in a consumerist society everyone is becoming consumers of various products that claim to be enriching their life in all possible ways. And certain products available in market become 'unavoidable' in one's day to-day family life, from children to adults. Especially in the Indian scenario, where family and its structure are given utmost importance, most of the advertisements revolve around a family setting. This is particularly evident in the portrayal of products basically aimed at children.

One of the most widely used nutritive products for children in the market is "Horlicks" and it claims to make every child who regularly drinks it, "taller", "stronger" and "sharper". The advertisement is well set against a family background. The advertisement focuses on a boy (interestingly girls were added much later to the ad) who is soon going to conduct an interview with a renowned scientist in India since his project was "the best" in the school. There comes the all-knowing mother who provides him with "the best" drink "Horlicks" which is backed up with the assurance of a doctor. Horlicks has never failed to show a mother (not a father) who takes care of the child and the male doctor who assures the credibility of the product.

On the surface, the advertisement succeeds in capturing the attention of all mothers who really care for their children. However, on closer analysis, this ad can be seen as a cultural text perpetuating existing domestic norm, by stereotyping the character of the mother. The family shown here is clearly an Indian family and the mother who appears on the screen from the inner room is a typical Indian mother as she wears a saree. The advertisement gives much importance to the gestures of the mother, her role, her actions, etc. as she is portrayed as listening to her kids amidst her chores. By finishing Rohan's sentence, the mother becomes someone who completely knows the child, carefully attending to his every need and all. The advertisement also captures the mother's facial expressions and the movement of her eyes when she thinks of her son's future achievements. It thus gives the picture of how an Indian mother is supposed to act. She is also presented as a gentle, soft woman in the house.

Throughout the advertisement, Rohan's father is not seen anywhere in the scene. He remains an absent father in the advertisement who leaves all the duties of bringing up a child to the mother alone. It is highly ironical that even though presented as an Indian family, which gives more importance to the father figure, the advertisement is portraying his absence. The primary aim of this ad, as that of all others, is to advertise the product but the visuals or scenes implicitly present how a typical Indian mother should be, how she alone is supposed to look after the child/children carefully by remaining within the four walls of the house. Her whole life, movements, dreams, etc. are limited or forcefully confined within the walls of the house itself, hardly capable of breaking away any of the existing norms. Even the recent ad of Horlicks only has mother and a boy in it, with an absent father.

Another product in the market that appeals better to the children is 'Kinder Joy' candies. The recent advertisement of this product which was well set again in a family scenario introduces the new edition of 'Kinder Schoko-Bons Crispy'. The mother who comes late to the living room finds everyone busy in their own world. Suddenly, she brings in the candy and tastes it in a manner that catches the attention of others to succeed in bringing every one near her and thus she fulfils the duty thrust upon her, the maintenance of unity in family. Even the caption of the candy goes similar to this, "the taste of togetherness". The whole family scene is intertwined with the visual description of the candy's complex structure.

Seeing through the lens, this mother is also the same but wears a kurti as opposed to saree. She was not with other when the scene opens and makes a late entry to find everyone around her, husband and children, busy. The dialogue she murmurs within, as an aside, emphatically reflects how Indian society expects the woman, the wife, the mother to behave in the family. She is considered as a factor or medium that unifies all others in the family. On the other hand, she is forced to restrict herself within the domestic boundaries. Even though she is bestowed with that duty to unite them together, she is supposed to find the solution from within the house, specifically from kitchen itself.

Towards the end of the advertisement, with the help of the candies she brings everyone to her and they start to share their moments of that day with the mother. This shows that the husband and children do not normally share their daily happenings with her. They consider her life to be within the kitchen, to cook for them, to meet their needs, etc. It seems that the mother is not considered as an individual with her own aspirations and dreams. She is getting more stereotyped by her husband and even by her children, the younger generation, whom we hopefully consider will change all the existing and discriminatory norms. She is merely reduced to the typical care-taker of the family. The first product of Kinder group, 'Kinder Joy', is very well gendered as they made a distinction between the candies for boys and girls, through its outer covering. The traditional colour association—blue for boys and pink for girls—is blindly reiterated. Similarly, the toy within it also varies; it is a car, a gun, a robot etc for the boy child within the blue pack, and a Barbie doll for the girl child, within the pink pack.

CONCLUSION

Advertisements are no more mere "intermission fillers". The underlying messages in each and every advertisement do have a profound hold on individual's thought process, perception, societal norms, religious and cultural values, and so on. Advertisements, in the process of its development itself, carry the "burden of guilt" (Nigam, 1) for treating women in a demeaning manner like depicting them as objects to meet out men's desire and comfort. The objectification of women in advertisements has drastically declined in recent years, but now it has taken to other ways to lower the status of women. In recent years advertisements have come up with the portrayal of the smart mom's independence and passion, the super wife's assertion in choice, and young girls' choice of education over marriage, etc. It is an undeniable fact that media and advertisements play a vital role in social conditioning, directly or indirectly.

A recent progressive change in the attitude towards women in advertisements is that even when they are represented as someone in the "background", serving family members, dutiful daughter-in-law, caring mothers etc., they are never disgraced or belittled as dumb, indecisive, sexual objects, victims of male desire etc. Far away from the representation in the traditional advertisements, the depiction of women in advertisements has changed a lot. In the past women were portrayed as economically dependent on men and to be taken care of throughout their life, echoing Manu's ideology. The change has mainly resulted from the increase in the educational levels of women, the "exposure to the West", and the influences from the various movements aimed at the liberation of women from the shackles of discrimination.

Shoma A. Chatterji's essays found the insidious impact of advertisements in "reinforcing patriarchal norms" (Nigam 77) through the representation of women in advertisements. Chatterji clearly states that "a stereotyped notion of gender roles is evident in the casting" of advertisements, where men are given roles of "demonstrators" and experts while women are given only "auxiliary roles" (Nigam, 77).

Literary circles now-a-days witness the emergence of radical feminist thinkers, the concept of new woman, etc. which confidently declares the complete independence of women. It is then highly paradoxical that the presentation of woman even in the shortest advertisement is very much in accordance with the patriarchal concepts. Through these advertisements the advertisers are trying to create "a mass culture" which is identical everywhere, that upholds Patriarchy and its norms. All the women in advertisements follow the same pattern, 'desirable' or 'satisfactory' in the man's world, though far more progressive than the old-fashioned representation of women as objects of pleasure.

Television advertisements go on harping about good mothers who feed their children with health drinks, ideal wives who cares about their husband's health, and even grand mothers who advise their daughter-in-laws etc. All such advertisements are reinforcing a lifestyle which confines the woman to household chores and make the man to be her master. By presenting only the more extreme stereotypes, advertisements tend to "underscore and reinforce the negative feelings many women have about themselves" (Nigam, 80). Through "institutionalizing -two-dimensional images of women" the media is making it harder for women to break the chains of their limitations.

WORKS CITED

Adorno, Theodor and Max Hokheimer. "The Culture Industry: Enlightenment as Mass

Deception." New York: Continuum, 1993. Web. 17 Dec 2016.

Akrani, Gaurav. "Pupose, Features, Advantages, Role and 5 M's of Advertising."

Kalyan City Life Blog. Kalyan City Life, 7 July 2010. Web. 20 Dec 2016. Baudrillard, Jean. The Consumer Society: Myths And Structure. London: Sage,

1998. Web. 10 Mar 2017.

Chatterji, Shoma A. "How Advertising Exploit Women?." Divya Nigam and

Jyotsna Jha. Ed. Women in Advertising: Changing Perspectives. Hyderabad: The Icfai UP, 2007. Print.

Fatihi, A. R. The Language of Advertising and TV Commercials. New Delhi: Bahri

Publications, 1991. Print.

Horlicks India. Advertisement. YouTube, 23 July 2015. Web. 17 Dec 2016. Kinder Schoko-

Bons Crispy. Advertisement. YouTube, 19 Sep 2016. Web. 17 Dec

2016

Nayar, Pramod. K. An Introduction to Cultural Studies. New Delhi: Viva Book Pvt.

Ltd., 2008. Print.

Nigam, Divya. "Women in Advertising: A Comparison between Western and Asian

Perspectives." Divya Nigam andJyotsna Jha. Ed. Women in Advertising: ChangingPerspectives. Hyderabad: The Icfai UP, 2007. Print.

Women in Advertising: Changing Perspectives. Divya Nigam and Jyotsna Jha. Ed.

Hyderabad: The Icfai UP, 2007. Print.

Williams, Raymond. "Advertising: the Magic System." Advertising And Society Review,

vol. 1 no. 1, 2000. Project Muse. Web. 20 Dec 2016

Wood, Julia T. "Gendered Media: The Influence of Media on Views of Gender." Google

Scholar. n.p. n.d. 31-41. Web. 20 Dec 2016

BIO-NOTE

Harsha Anna Kuriakose, previously served as a Guest Lecturer in KVVS College of Science and Technology, Adoor, is a Senior Customer Service Specialist in iEnergizer IT Service Pvt Ltd., Noida. Still carrying her lover for Literature, she spends her leisure time in writing poetry and other art and craft works. Finding happiness from her surroundings and writing keeps her moving forward in her hectic customer centric world.

CHAPTER XI

SPEAKING OUT THE UNSPOKEN: RE-WRITING THE OLD SCHEMA OF MALAYALAM MOVIES IN THE TWENTY FIRST CENTURY

Jeelu Elsa Thampi

ABSTRACT

Malayalam movie scenario has undergone great changes in the course of its evolution. Films focusing on love, politics and family life have changed to films of contemporary relevance that make people think and discuss in a serious as well as satirical manner. With the arrival of postmodernism in cinema, the fields of exploration moved beyond its usual spectrum. The 'otherness' came to be discussed. The representation of the subaltern, their 'unseen' pining and denial of the rights of the downtrodden gained more attention. The issues of chastity, gender, sexuality, caste and class came to be discussed in the movies. The so-called notions of the 'unspoken' subjects like sex, homosexuality, violence, exploitation of children and rape came to be represented in Malayalam movies. The issues of women empowerment and that of the third gender widely gained prominence in the movies that were released in the post 2010 period. The paper discusses how Malayalam movies have evolved from time to time in terms of their themes and relevance by incorporating novel ideas and also by questioning the old scheme of matters presented in the previous generation of movies.

Keywords: Otherness, Gender, Homosexuality, Politics, Women empowerment and Subaltern.

Speaking out the Unspoken: Re-Writing the Old Schema of Malayalam Movies in the Twenty First Century.

• • •

INTRODUCTION

Movies are thought to be one of the most powerful media of expression. They are capable of communicating through visual and aural elements. The darkness of the movie theatre brings to light the thought awakening process of the spectator. Movies make things quickly get registered in human thoughts. The central narrator of each movie is its camera lens. Through this lens the spectator explores the world of the characters and the dimensions of their narratives. Earlier, movies tried to communicate the direct meaning of what they intended to convey. But the modern as well as postmodern movies try to incorporate an indirect element which the viewers are expected to decrypt. The twenty first century Indian movies try to bring about innovative changes in their presentation including changes in themes, colour tones, modes of meaning conveyance etc.

Indian movie scenario has undergone great changes in the course of its evolution. Indian movie industry has started to experiment in its style with the onset of the twenty first century. This experimentation is visible in the designing of titles, characters, songs, production and other technical aspects. The paper mainly focuses attention on the changes that occurred in Indian cinema, stressing mainly on Malayalam films. Films focusing on love, politics and family life have changed to films of contemporary relevance that make people think and discuss in a serious as well as satirical manner. Earlier Indian movies depicted patriarchy that instructed how hierarchy in family should be respected and the way people were obliged to follow the submissive traditions. The influence of religion and morality were seen greatly in such films.

Malayalam films have changed drastically in its approach towards sticking on to traditional way of thinking. There are a lot of movies which question the current status of affairs in the society. People have started to think through questioning the various ideologies presented in the movies. Soap-drama movies are not much welcome these days. Through movies, the governing bodies of state and nation, the institutions such as family, religion, education etc. are being questioned. In a way, movies are educating common people to change the traditional norms and adapt themselves into a new culture.

Kevin McDonald in his work *Film Theory: The Basics* discusses about the changes that occurred in the movie industry:

By the end of the twentieth century, the meaning of film had become more complicated. In some ways, film has become more diffuse, merging with competing technologies like television, video games, and the internet. The proliferation of these technologies has certainly changed the ways in which films are circulated and consumed.... Film's complexity is not just the result of the changing material or discursive status, but part of its overall standing as a cultural object. Film has always been intertwined with the paradoxical implications of modern life or what is sometimes more generally called modernity.... [...] film is prized for its verisimilitude and its ability to document physical reality. It is taken to be a factual, trustworthy source of evidence, and a paragon of realist representation. On the other hand, film is characterised as an optical illusion and a celebrated source of entertainment best known for its fictional scenarios. In this regard, film is closely associated with its ability to elicit pleasure and its affinity with fantasy and distortion. These different attributes have all prompted elaborate debates about film's social and psychological effects. (iii-iv)

REPRESENTATION OF THE 'OTHERNESS'

With the introduction of postmodernism in Indian cinema, the notions of freedom of thought and communication gained a different meaning. The fields of exploration moved beyond its usual spectrum. The notion of 'otherness' came to be discussed in the movies. The issue of 'genderraceclasssexuality', a portmanteau term put forth by Robyn Wiegman is seriously taken into consideration by the moviemakers. The marginalisation that occurs due to one's gender, race, class and sexuality are issues that bear all-time relevance. Women, children, the third gender and the lower stratum of the society are always categorised as the 'other' in literature and movies. The helplessness of these 'weaker' sections and the exploitative nature of the upper class are portrayed in the twenty first century. The representation of the subaltern, their 'unseen' pining and denial of the rights of the downtrodden gained more attention. The so-called notions of the 'unspoken' subjects like sex, virginity, homosexuality, violence, exploitation of children and rape came to be represented in Indian movies. All these aspects are more or the less factors that 'victimise' the 'other'.

As a Third World nation like India, where people still adhere to the colonial mentalities, twenty first century movies explore the areas where such colonial mentalities thrive. The socially and economically backward communities are explored much in this respect. Movies like *Jana Gana Mana* (2022), *Puzhu* (2022), *Kammattipaadam* (2016), *Thottappan* (2019), *Kismath* (2016), Aanum Pennum (2021) and *Bheeshma Parvam* (2022) discuss the issues of casteism, honour killing and betrayal. These movies show the way certain people are marginalized on the basis of their caste and race. The difficulty of the upper-class people in accepting the 'coloured' man is still a valid issue. In such movies, it is clearly seen how the rights of these people are brutally denied when they question any injustice they face. This can be seen in movies like *Kammattippadam* (2016), *Ee.Ma.Yau.* (2018), etc.

The character of Gangadharan/ Ganga played by Vinayakan in *Kammattippppadam* and the character of Eeshi played by Chemban Vinod in *Ee.Ma.Yau.* are brilliant examples of the exploited community who are denied of their basic rights. It is their financial instability and social backwardness that make them vulnerable to the fag end of their deprived selves. Ganga gets killed at the end whereas Eeshi is denied of the burial ceremony of his father in the church, having to dig out the six feet grave by himself in their own compound. In *Puzhu* (2022), the protagonist murders his pregnant sister and her husband in the name of casteism. In *Happy Sardar* (2021), the younger brother, trying uphold the honour of his religion, attempts to kill the elder sister when she elopes with a

Muslim.

INFLUENCE OF WESTERN CULTURE AND LIFE STYLE

There is a strong tendency of imitating the Western life and culture and this gets mockingly or satirically represented in the twenty first century Indian movies. The dressing style, food, technological advancements and addiction to Western products get exquisitely portrayed in such movies. The depiction of the life of male emigrants in movies like *ABCD* (2013) and *Life of Josootty* (2015) are stark contrasts between the rich and the poor trying to establish a living in the Western countries. Women in such movies are represented as bold characters overpowering or betraying men. In movies like *My Boss* (2012), *Two Countries* (2015) and *Njan Prakashan* (2018), the male characters woo for the hands of the female characters out of their intense desire to enter into the Western nations in the prospect of accumulating wealth and social status rather than out of true love.

PORTRAYAL OF WOMEN AND CHILDREN AS EMPOWERED AND VICTIMISED

Indian movies in the present era still have an affinity towards portraying women as objects of sexual gratification. The use of violence and brutal rape against women are used as major tools in trying to subjugate women. Through such an act, the overpowering female character is 'moralised' by men. The voyeuristic pleasure and the inherent brute nature suppressed in human psyche gets exposed in such portrayals. Movies like *Puthiya Niyamam* (2016), *Theevram* (2012), *Ira* (2018), *22 Female Kottayam* (2012), *Queen* (2018), *Vaashi* (2022)etc. portray the female protagonists as the 'victims' of rape. The binary construction of victim-victimiser comes into play in these movies. It is, again mostly, the male characters who seek revenge against the victimiser.

A major change to be noted is that in the movie *Queen* (2017), the makers present some open questions that is left for the spectators to ponder about. It presents the question to the spectators whether there exists an 'odd time' for women. Women who walk in the streets at late night either due to their late work schedule or quest for independence are usually stereotyped as immoral. But none of these apply to men and they enjoy absolute freedom. Even children are not spared from sexual violence depicted in movies. Movies like *Pathaam Valavu* (2022), *The Great Father* (2017), *5 Sundarikal* (2013), *Palunku* (2006) and *Aagathan* (2010)show school-going girls undergoing the traumatic experience of rape. The question of 'hushed up' topics like chastity or virginity are also discussed in movies like *96* (2018), *22 Female Kottayam*, etc.

The topic of women empowerment also gets discussed in several movies like *How Old Are You?* (2014), *Mili* (2015), *Udaaharanam Sujatha* (2017), *June* (2018)etc. Not only do the movies render women emerging out of the domestic chores to the public domain, but also learning to deal with the tormentors who let them down. This is explicit in the character of Tessa played by Rima Kallingal to her recruiting agent Cyril whose role is played by Fahad Fazil in *22 Female Kottayam*. The female protagonists of Malayalam movies are mostly depicted as bold characters who can strongly say 'no' to whoever they think might let them down. The character Devi played by Samyuktha Menon in *Theevandi* (2018)is bold enough to slap her fiancé Bineesh Damodaran, whose role is taken up by Tovino Thomas, for many a time for being a chain smoker. Shahana in *Usthad Hotel* (2012) is ready to break apart her engagement with Mehroof due to the overpowering nature that blinds him.

Movies like *Freedom Fight* (2022), *Sara's* (2021), *The Great Indian Kitchen* (2021), *Ramante Edenthottam* (2017), *Uyare* (2019), *Take Off* (2017), *Biriyani* (2020) etc. explore the areas where women are restricted in family and how they tackle those restrictive webs to break the shackles of confinement in order to pursue their dreams. Here, gender roles are being questioned. Here, the familial roles of women- that is, women as child bearers, objects of sexual gratification and exploitation, someone whose life is always confined to complete the household chores, somebody whose dreams and aspirations are suppressed for the upliftment of the family- are brought to the limelight in a different perspective.

Women's rights are truly enforced through these movies by portraying their status in family and society and how they become the victims of oppression and abuse.

DEPICTION OF THE THIRD GENDER AND THEIR SEXUALITY

The issues of the third gender, homosexuality, etc. that were once categorised as tabooed topics in the Indian context are now taken up by the twenty first century directors. Movies like *My Life Partner* (2014), *Mumbai Police* (2013), *Achaayans* (2017) and *Moothon* (2019)discuss the topic of homosexuality. Jayasurya's lead character in *Njan Marykkutty* (2018), a movie based on the transsexual communitywas well accepted by the spectators and this shows the transformed mentality of the spectators who have learned to accept the society as it is.

VISUALISATION OF POLITICS, VIOLENCE AND TERRORISM IN MOVIES

Violence of politics and rewriting of the past histories are now taken as big budget movies. The huge settings and the resultant hundred crore plus- income movies capture the attention of the spectators. *Kaayamkulam Kochunni* (2018), etc. display the extensive film settings that costed crores of money as well as grossed more than the production cost after its premiering. The action-oriented movies also gained much popularity. Films like *Pulimurugan* (2016), *Odiyan* (2018), *Lucifer* (2019), etc. are perfect examples of action-oriented movies that grossed crores. All these movies indirectly promote violence in human nature. People tend to imitate such deeds of violence in real life.

A perfect example of such a movie is *Drishyam* (2013)where violence or killing and distortion of truth are promoted. More than three cases have been reported in Kerala that followed the *Drishyam* model killing and destruction of evidences. Power politics gets indirectly represented through movies. *Passenger* (2009) and *Left Right Left* (2013) are perfect examples of such movies where the corruption and power play combine to reveal the worst side of politics. The themes of religious fanaticism and terrorism also bring out violence in the movies like *Anwar* (2010) and *B.Tech* (2018). There again, the viewers are addressed with another topic to think whether every Muslim be brought under the suspicion of being a terrorist instead of a single person or a group of peoples' evil thoughts and deeds.

Post 2010 has witnessed a lot of psychopath movies whereby serial killings and the investigation related to them have become common topics. A western influence can be seen here. *Memories* (2013) was a pathbreaking movie in such an aspect. *Grandmaster* (2012), *Masters* (2012), *Anjaam Paathira* (2020), *Forensic* (2020), *21 Grams* (2022) and *Paappan* (2022) are some of the examples of the psychopath movies in Malayalam industry which expose a series of psychopath killings for some or no reason.

QUESTIONING THE VARIOUS POLICIES

Movies like *Jana Gana Mana* (2022), *Naayaattu* (2021), *One* (2021), *Nirnaayakam* (2015) etc. question the various policies of central and state governments. It features the pressures that government officials face in implementing the laws. These movies also portray the areas where the government has failed in ensuring the rights and also suggests various corrective measures. Some of these questions are very relevant which every common man wishes to raise to the law implementing bodies. Because at times, they too feel that their rights are denied and the feelings of the common man are not being valued much. Characters in movies like *Pathaam Valavu* (2022), *Drishyam* (2014), *Vaashi* (2022), *21 Grams* (2022) etc. take the initiative to serve justice on their own when they find that justice is not being rightly served to them. Often, we see that the higher authorities close their eyes to many injustices. At these points, movies function as eye-openers to raise public consciousness.

PORTRAYAL OF MEDIA AND CYBERCRIMES

The corruptive influence of media and technology in modern lives and its consequences are clearly shown in movies like *Operation Java* (2021), *Keedam* (2022), *Android Kunjappan Version 5.25* (2019), *12th Man* (2022) and *C U Soon* (2020). The competitive world of media channels is exposed through movies like *Run Baby Run* (2012), *Naradan* (2022), *Night Drive* (2022) and *Love 24×7* (2015). In these movies, the present-day manipulation and misinterpretation of news items, the pressure and frustration of journalists and their attempts to bring out truth are very well portrayed.

The transaction of ideas has become a bit more connotative these days. Sometimes the audience need to watch a movie once again to understand the implied meaning conveyed through various scenes and dialogues. Each dialogue and object speak to the audience in a clear manner. At the same time, double meaning poses a threat to small children as they automatically include the cuss words and obscenities somewhere in their area of communication in their day to day lives. There is a need to censor such scenes of visual and verbal obscenities in movies.

FILM SONGS AS A MEDIUM OF EXPRESSION

Finally, changes are brought about in the presentation of the titles and songs. Titles are designed innovatively in the twenty first century Malayalam movies. The peculiarity of the design of the title bears symbolic significance. For example, the title font design of *Premam* (2015) has the shape of a butterfly, and butterflies can be seen in the three phases of the protagonist's life. Songs also have their own significance. The older songs are reworked into latest trend for a new experience of listening. Sometimes songs are introduced with a revolutionary intention that has an element of protest or awareness to convey to the people. For example, the song "Parudeesa" from *Bheeshma Parvam* (2022), "Eamanmare eamanmare..." from *Oru Mexican Apaaratha* (2017) and "Nottam" from *Sarvopari Palakkaran* (2017)are two such examples that portray the protest against the societal norms and customs. "Kaala perum kaala" from *Sherlock Toms* (2017) and "Mazha varunnunde" from *Thattumpurath Achuthan* (2018)are two such examples that portray awareness to the people. Rap songs are also being popular in Malayalam movies and albums to communicate radical ideas.

CONCLUSION

To conclude, the twenty first century Malayalam movies brought about a different perspective of narration by speaking about the unspoken notions that were not so far discussed in the South Indian context. A revolution has been made out of films in India that try to etch a new history that retells the cultures and lives we see around us.

WORKS CITED

Dix, Andrew. "Films and Ideology." *Beginning Film Studies.* Manchester UP, 2016, pp. 226-268.

McDonald, Kevin. "Introduction". *Film Theory: The Basics.* Routledge, 2016, pp. iii-iv.

BIO-NOTE

Jeelu Elsa Thampi is a higher secondary school guest teacher at St. Thomas Higher Secondary School, Kozhencherry. She hails from Kozhencherry. She completed her B. A. in English Language and Literature from Assumption College, Changanacherry, M.A. in English Literature from Mar Thoma College, Tiruvalla and B.Ed. in English Education from Titus II Teachers College, Tiruvalla. She is interested in writing poems and reviewing movies. She participated in the Kerala State Youth Festival and bagged 'A' grade for essay and versification in English consecutively in 2013 and 2014.

THE NAMESAKE: DISOWNING ONE'S REALITY

Parvathy Varma M. A.

ABSTRACT

Jhumpa Lahiri's *The Namesake* is such a work in Literature where the fictional characters are people we have come across in life or in a few situations, we ourselves. It is a reality check for human beings on how people actually disown themself, i.e., their reality. The paper is an attempt to critically analyze this tendency shown by almost all characters in the novel. Indian diasporic writers were always amused by cultural conflict and this has been reflected in their works. Lahiri has also made use of the same but her characters do not always fall into archetypes. The Namesake is a narrative about an Indian Bengali family who migrated to America for future prospects. The novel throws light on the identity crisis of migrants as they move from their place to a foreign land. The hindrances, struggles, and hopes challenge these people to stay true to themselves.

Keywords: Reality, Identity, Culture, and Migrants.

The Namesake: Disowning One's Reality.

• • •

Literature is an expression, an expression of freedom, identity, and being true to oneself. It was and will always be the most acceptable way of connecting to human beings; as Literature, for the most part, is life itself. Coated in a fancy world of fiction does not keep literature at bay.

The Namesake is the debut novel of renowned writer and translator, Jhumpa Lahiri. She received Pulitzer Prize in 2000 for Interpreter of Maladies. It is a story of culture, inheritance, customs, race, and migration and how these factors can affect the direct lives of people. The novel was critically acclaimed for its discussion of identity crisis and cultural conflict.

Inheritance is something we all are acquainted with, in some or the other way. The place where we were born, the society in which we grew up and its culture is always influential in either way. A typical Indian Bengali family is being more or less forced to be displaced from this and to settle their lives in a new land, in between new people and an entirely different culture. This indeed can lead to an identity crisis in each of them but in *The Namesake*, this eventually leads them to a phase of disowning their reality in multiple situations.

When Ashima and Ashoke Ganguli move to the United States of America for a better future, they might not have thought about how their identity would question and at some point, they may have to compromise their reality for survival. In the opening of the novel, which is set in 1968, Ashima is carrying and misses her hometown and its local snacks. From the following pages, it is clear that Ashima is lonely and has to fight her mind every day to keep herself happy and indeed, sane. The first part of the novel concentrates mostly on Ashima and her emotions. The way she misses the comfort of her home, her parents, and the insecurity she felt in the new land. Being a typical Indian woman, she finds it difficult to fluently speak the English language or to confidently face any foreigner. In the very beginning, Lahiri makes an account of Ashima's typical Indian mindset by saying, "Like a kiss or caress in a Hindi movie, a husband's name is something intimate and therefore unspoken, cleverly patched over" (2). Even at the time of her delivery and afterward, she is not able to recognize her true self nor she is able to place herself in her current reality.

Ashoke Ganguli is more or less free from a lot of identity crises when compared to other characters in the novel. He always wanted to go abroad and make a better future for himself, listening to his intelligent grandfather. Ashoke is a person who can accept things on his journey of life and this may have been a result of his moribund experience while traveling to his grandparents. He has faced his death and migrating to a country is nothing compared to that. This might have given him the strength to face his realities. But even then, when he realized that his children are nothing like their parents, but completely attached to the foreign land they were born and brought up in, this installed in him a fear of facing his reality. Though Ashoke was always interested in reading English books and knowing their culture, he never preferred it over his. When his children did not understand the importance of the culture and customs he and his wife have followed throughout their life, he finds it unacceptable.

When their son Gogol, the carrier of their family name finds it difficult to accept his name and live with it, the novel evolves itself into another domain of human concerns. A name may sound quite insignificant for most of us because we never found it difficult to accept the name given to each of us by our parents or the society we grew up in, but for Gogol, his name could never do justice to his real self and he hated being Gogol all through his life. Even when he was Gogol every day, when he had to live with it, he was not being himself and he refused to accept his reality. Gogol becomes Nikhil at one point in the novel but this does not change the fact that he disowned his reality. His name was not merely a reflection of his crisis but also a reflection of the dilemma he faced throughout his life.

Sonia, the daughter of Ashoke and Ashima is a subtle character throughout the novel. The identity crisis she felt is much more subtle than others because she was born into a family where they almost accepted the way their life is led to. She was named once and she was able to accept it, this solved half her problems, unlike Gogol. She was confident in her actions, and her decisions, especially in her love life, where Gogol failed miserably. She might possibly be the only major character in the novel who is not much discussed but plays a major role in the life of other characters. She is neither proud of her inheritance nor ashamed of it. She does not hate her life nor is extremely excited about it.

There are a few other characters who are introduced by the author in different situations in the lives of different characters. But they are not facing the crisis of having an identity for themselves, rather they are able to accept their lives as they are. Gogol's wife Moushumi is a good example of this. Though she faces dilemmas, she lives according to her heart. She does not feel ashamed to have an extramarital affair nor is sticking to her so-called cultural values. She, even though was attracted to Gogol in the beginning and wanted to spend the rest of her life with him, she eventually lost it. She is able to accept that reality about her. Gogol in the same situation tries to escape again from his existence. Gogol's girlfriend Maxine, who is a foreigner is also able to move on from him easily. We can recognize these particular events in Gogol's life as an eye-opener to him. Towards the end of the novel, even though Gogol seems to have finally accepted his reality, the author mentions, "...anxious to return to his room, to be alone..." (290). This shows that he still wanted to escape from his current existence to a world of his own.

"I hate the name Gogol," he says. "I've always hated it" (102). The reason Gogol says the judge to change his name to Nikhil is a prominent one and is a milestone in the novel not only because Gogol does not admit it to his parents, but he is unable to accept his whole life. Gogol is his existence but Nikhil is his expected reality. The journey from Gogol to Nikhil is expected to bring him back his love for life and himself, and to accept everything about him. But "...everyone he knows in the world still calls him Gogol. He is aware that his parents, and their friends, and the children of their friends, and all his own friends from high school, will never call him anything but Gogol" (103).

Later in life, Gogol is rather pushing himself to be Nikhil and he is bothered about it until he meets Maxine. His life takes a turn when love hits him. He falls for Maxine, an American girl, not just because she was attractive but because it was his wish to escape from his Indian reality. He always hated the customs and traditions his family ritually followed and did not want to be a part of them.

So, when he falls for Maxine, he is majorly attracted to her way of living and the freedom she has to make her own decisions. He is surprisingly shocked by the way her parents are, how they are unbothered about the way Maxine lives and he is happy seeing them live for themselves rather than their daughter, which is exactly the opposite of his parents.

At one point when Gogol explains about his life, Maxine is surprised to hear certain things about his life. "...that all his parents' friends are Bengali, that they had had an arranged marriage, that his mother cooks Indian food every day, that she wears saris and a bindi. "Really?" she says, not fully believing him" (138). Though Maxine is surprised by these facts, Gogol is rather ashamed of these facts. He is not proud of his existence and he always wanted to change everything about it. His pretension of reality makes Maxine say "But you're so different. I would never have thought that" (138). Maxine, seeing his ways have always thought of him as American and she couldn't accept otherwise. "To him, the terms of his parents' marriage are something at once unthinkable and unremarkable...but their lives bear no resemblance to that of Gerald and Lydia..." (138). When Maxine asks him whether his parents would want him to marry an Indian girl, he feels angry at his parents, wishing they could be otherwise, he still refuses to accept his reality by saying "I don't know," he tells her. "I guess so. It doesn't matter what they want" (139).

When Maxine's parents refer to him as 'Nick' and forgets that he is Indian, he doesn't get offended but confused. He has had this confusion all his life, he wishes for a life he is not given and is not able to accept his current scenarios. Each of the incidents in the novel between Gogol and Maxine is a perfect example of how he wants to change his way of living to something entirely different. Sometimes he is even ashamed to talk about his parents, their concerns, their way of living, and their customs. He dresses American, he listens to English Music and everything about the foreign land as he has always thought of it as something superior to his own culture.

The names in the novel depict a huge part of the cultural identity they hold. They wanted to be included as Indians in America and not as Americans. While Ashoke and Ashima are proud of their names, Gogol wants to escape from them. For that, he becomes Nikhil and in so many situations, Nick. That change had given him a sense of security in least at some situations of his life. Though Gogol was named after the famous Russian writer Nikolai Gogol, he sees his name as bound to a backward, traditional Bengali heritage which he never feels belonged. Though he tries to run away as far as possible from everything he is born to, he helplessly bounces back to the same. This scenario is not rare among immigrants. They feel inferior to the society and its culture to which they have moved to. They feel the American culture is much superior to theirs and they feel insecure in a capitalist society. They feel a need deep inside to improve their way of living so that they feel included. Gogol in the novel feels the same as he has a strong sense of inferiority towards the society in which he lives.

Though Ashima is equally insecure about her life in the new land, her character has a worthy justification for it. Ashima was born and brought up in India, in a middle-class family and it was normal for her to feel insecure in a modern, free society. Still, Ashima does not completely give up on her reality and she holds on to it as much as she can. She feels inferior to wear sari and communicating in English but she never compromises her Indian reality for their family's American dream. She disowns her reality at a different level when she loses her husband. After her husband's demise, she wants to move back to India but something pulls her back each time. She knows her heart doesn't belong where she lives anymore, but in her native, yet, she refuses to accept it for a long time. She was concerned about her children but that cannot be a justification for her crisis because her children were grown up and independent. Ashima finally copes with her existence and moves to India towards the end of the novel and this is indeed an evolution of a character from an insecure, dependent woman to an independent decision-maker. When she says "Remember when we used to put on those awful flashing colored lights?... I didn't know a thing back then" (285), we know how life has treated her. When Gogol introduces Maxine to his parents and takes her home, he is reluctant and insecure about his family. He tells her that they can't behave intimately in front of his parents nor there will be any wine for lunch. He describes his household and all these with a tinge of hate. He somehow wants to get done with Maxine meeting his parents and wants to escape into another world with her.

After his father's demise, Gogol has few realizations about himself and his family but this is short-lived. His marriage with Moushumi failed more or less due to his unacceptance of himself as a person. A person should always be proud of his existence which Gogol is not. He finds his solace in others but that doesn't give him peace. He is ultimately not himself throughout the narration. Moushumi's extramarital affair is quite shocking to him but he feels numb. He straight away asks her:

Are you having an affair?" The question had sprung out of him, something he had not consciously put together in his mind until that moment. It felt almost comic to him, burning in his throat. But as soon as he asked it, he knew. He felt the chill of her secrecy, numbing him, like a poison spreading quickly through his veins. He'd felt this way on only one other occasion, the night he had sat in the car with his father and learned the reason for his name" (282).

This instance is one of the most beautifully narrated parts of the novel. A person finding out what he thinks nor experiences is his reality is astonishing and Lahiri here has done justice to the same. Gogol realizes his name, which he had hated throughout, has the value of his father's life, and his wife, whom he loved very much cheating on him has the same effect on his mind. He goes numb in both situations because both are altering his reality, which he has refused to accept.

According to a critic, "Because the Ganguli's carry with them myriad traditions and practices upon migrating to the United States, their son finds it difficult to establish himself in society and find his own identity" (Terry-Ann Dawes). Gogol thus tries to include himself in both worlds, but miserably fails in it and ultimately ends up disowning his reality.

The unending search for identity is a common theme in such novels but Lahiri here has explored different levels of it. Her characters not only search for their identity but disowns their reality, especially Gogol, whom we can refer to as the protagonist of the novel. He is a reflection of people around us as human beings have a normal tendency to run away from their reality in order to escape from the sadness or dilemma it causes and they try to create a parallel, happy existence for themselves but this does not make them feel any better is the truth. Escaping from situations and people cannot lead to happiness and it is quite clear through the narrative.

WORKS CITED

Lahiri, Jhumpa. The Namesake. Harper Collins, 2019. Print

Dawes, Terr-Ann. "The Namesake: A Struggle for identity." 18 Oct. 2016. Web. 26 Sept.

2022. https://nsuworks.nova.edu/mako/vol1/iss1/2/

BIO-NOTE

Parvathy Varma is a postgraduate in English Literature from Bharathiar University. She completed her graduation in English language and Literature from the University of Calicut. Her areas of interest include fiction, cultural studies, poetry, and movies. She specializes in oration and article writing. She is inspired by her parents, teachers, and great writers of all time.

CHAPTER XIII

A STUDY ON THE EFFECTIVENESS OF ONLINE FOODING APPS ON REGISTERED RESTAURANTS IN ALAPPUZHA DISTRICT WITH SPECIAL REFERENCE TO SWIGGY AND ZOMATO.

Sejin Philip George

ABSTRACT

This paper tries to analyse the role and influence of mobile applications in food delivery business. In this modern technological era, online food apps and their usage are very much a part of man's busy lifestyle. All they need to do is a single tap on their mobile phone screen and food will reach their doorsteps. Online business is also mandatory for any food production company to flourish; with timely updations. The study focuses primarily on analysing the effectiveness of online restaurant food apps in terms of their low cost, sales, corporate image, etc.

Keywords: E-Commerce, Made to Order (MTO), Online Food Apps, and Sales.

A Study on the Effectiveness of Online Fooding Apps on Registered Restaurants in Alappuzha District with Special Reference to Swiggy and Zomato.

• • •

INTRODUCTION

The internet has become one of the most powerful forms of media in this technology- driven age. As traditional media consumption is declining, and online media consumption is growing, businesses need to change their way of operating. The younger generation is one of the reasons for increasing online media consumption. Many leading companies have begun to adopt online business strategies in order to revive from declining sales. Online business methods have also been implemented by restaurant companies. Several new restaurant companies are now offering Made to Order (MTO) food without a physical store. The online platform is used by such restaurants as a means to connect with their customers. In order to increase sales, the internet also provided the same benefits to traditional restaurants.

The internet has also led to the creation of "intermediaries" for restaurant companies, such as food ordering and delivery companies. Such intermediaries create partnerships with restaurants and list on their online platform the associated restaurants (i.e., mobile application websites). On the online platform, customers can then position their orders. These intermediaries' income is generated either through restaurant commission fees, customer delivery fees, or both. Online food apps enable customers to create a food delivery platform by expanding their choice and convenience with a single tap of their mobile phones to order from a wide range of restaurants. Online food apps provide the restaurants with a great platform by stabilizing their sales and sustaining their business. Whether the restaurants are big or small, they all try to get a piece of cake.

In the digital age, it is absolutely essential for every business to have an online presence whether it is a website, an e-commerce platform, a social media page or a combination of all the three helps the business in reaping major benefits. Even if the company does not conduct business online, customers and potential customers are expecting to see them online. In this modern era, every business is essential to establish an online platform for their business which will help them to get an opportunity of increasing their strong customer base and get the word out their business.

FOODING APPS COVERED UNDER THE STUDY

- Company Profile of Swiggy

Swiggy is a leading food ordering and delivery startup in India. The company started operations in 2014 and is headquartered in Bengaluru. Swiggy works by acting as a bridge between customers and restaurants. It utilizes an innovative technology platform that allows customers to order food from nearby restaurants and get it delivered at their doorstep. With Swiggy, customers do not have to keep the contact numbers of various restaurants and eateries in their locality. Swiggy works as a single point of contact for ordering food from all restaurants that may be there at a particular location. Swiggy has its own team of delivery professionals who pickup orders from restaurants and deliver it at the customer's doorstep. This has made the task of ordering food a lot easier for customers. Restaurants also gain by getting more orders and avoiding costs and efforts associated with maintaining their own delivery personnel.

The Business Mode of Swiggy
Swiggy has two major revenue streams:

- The major part of Swiggy's revenue is from commission it collects from restaurants for lead generation and for serving as a delivery partner.
- Swiggy also charges a nominal delivery fee from customers on orders below a threshold value which 200 rupees for most cities.

Marketing Strategies of Swiggy
Swiggy's marketing strategy consists of both online and offline marketing campaigns. It promotes its campaigns via Facebook, Twitter, YouTube, Pinterest, and Instagram. Some of its campaigns include 'Second to mom', #DiwaliGhayAayi, #SingwithSwiggy and 'Know your food' series of pictures and food walks in a local area. The company has successfully built its brand awareness and connects with its audience through these channels. Their Facebook page is quite active with regular updates, averaging to one post a day. Swiggy uses its social media not only for campaigning but to engage with its customers from solving the grievances to taking the feedback.

- **Company Profile of Zomato**

Zomato is an Indian restaurant search and discovery service founded in 2008 by Deepinder Goyal and Pankaj Chaddah. It currently operates in twenty-four countries. It provides information and reviews of restaurants, including images of menus where the restaurant does not have its own website and also online delivery services in some countries.

Marketing Strategy of Zomato

- Featured and user-friendly website
- Global mobile app
- Focus on digital marketing channels for potential customers
- Acquire the competitors: to be the largest resource in food supply market
- Zomato bought urban spoon for $52 million to enter US, Canada and Australia.
- Simpler review and rating system

BENEFITS OF FOOD DELIVERY APPLICATIONS

- Easy to use

The food ordering mobile apps are easy to use and offers high convenience with time and effort saving for the customers. This has encouraged more users to use the mobile apps and order their favorite food online to get them delivered to their houses.

- Flexible payments

The food ordering mobile apps offer flexible payment options for the customers to be able to pay using various modes of payments, best suitable for them.

- Real time tracking

The food ordering software is equipped with real time GPS tracking systems, such that the customers can track the delivery boy bringing their food, along with helping the delivery boys to track down the exact address of the customers.

- Loyalty points

Online food ordering often offers loyalty points to the customers for encouraging them to use the mobile app even more often. These loyalty points can be used by the customers to place future orders, thus helping them to use the app more often.

- Effective customer support

With 24/7 customer support facilities, the mobile apps can offer the best customer supports, answering to their queries and assisting them in any need or complaints.

EFFECTS OF FOOD DELIVERY APPS ON RESTAURANTS

- **POSITIVES**

1. **It is just one click away**

Today, more than ever, people can easily order online thanks to the Smartphone's and tablets. Studies conducted by the Interactive Advertising Bureau and Viggle show that about 69% of customers order food online using a mobile device. Whether on a break, stuck in traffic, or riding the bus, virtually anyone will place an order quickly and painlessly. In fact, this is a better and highly desirable alternative to waiting until getting home and placing the order over the phone.

2. It is fast, easy and comfortable

Customers choose to order food online because it is literally at their fingertips; fast, easy and comfortable. Virtually, anyone with a smart phone can order food online from a restaurant.

- **NEGATIVES**

Even though the demand for online fooding apps is high, the outlook for fine dining restaurants is strong because they place a premium on taste, while new ordering and delivery platforms mainly focus on convenience and price, the delivery business is

growing so fast, it is giving restaurants cause to rethink their expansion strategies too.

OBJECTIVES OF THE STUDY

- To study how effectively restaurants manage the cost of products delivered via food apps.
- To know the impact on sales after online food apps have been introduced.
- To study whether the restaurants' corporate image has improved through the use of technology.

SIGNIFICANCE OF THE STUDY

With the rapid growth of internet usage and related technologies, there are several opportunities on the web. As a result of the internet, so many firms and companies now enter their business with comfort. An online food ordering system is one of the businesses introduced by the internet. Many restaurants in today's life have focused on fast preparation and order delivery rather than offering a rich dining experience. Most of these delivery orders have been placed on the phone recently. It is therefore more relevant to explore how far these web applications are used by restaurants to reach their customers in order to make effective use of the online food delivery system. The study focuses primarily on analyzing the effectiveness of online restaurant food apps in terms of their low cost, sales, and corporate image.

DATA ANALYSIS AND INTERPRETATION

Findings of the Study:

1. The study found out that among these online applications in Alappuzha, Zomato is preferred by most of the restaurants.
2. The study also reveals that almost all the restaurants provide variety of food products such as South Indian, North Indian, Arabian, etc. along with juices and smoothies according to the needs of the customers through online media.
3. It is observed that most of the restaurants state that they incur service cost more for serving the customer needs. The respondents state that these costs are affordable for providing online services along with direct delivery.
4. Total cost involved in offering product using online food delivery application has moderately increased.
5. Through the introduction of the online food delivery system, the number of orders which they received had increased and there by sales also have increased.
6. Majority of the restaurants get a turnover, that has been a boost in the annual turnover of these restaurants, as such delivery applications have resulted in increasing the customer base and thus led to the growth in sales.
7. Majority of the restaurants pay commission at a considerable rate.
8. The study revealed that as the sales have increased, there is a difference in the margin of profits of the restaurants.
9. The study highlights that the Zomato app offers services at a low cost and that helps restaurants to get more orders thereby increasing sales.
10. Majority of the restaurants uses promotional techniques for increasing sales through social media, television, etc. in low cost.
11. The study observes that majority of the restaurants' corporate image has been enhanced after registering on these online food delivery applications.

SUGGESTIONS

1. Service providers should ensure timely upgradation of the online food delivery applications.
2. Communication systems should be improved between the delivery app executives and the restaurant owners.
3. Proper training must be ensured to the delivery assistants as their timely and prompt transference of ordered food to the customers have a great influence on successful running of such applications.
4. Keen attention must be given to the details of the order taken from the customers as error-free services are expected by customers through the usage of such apps.
5. The online delivery applications must be made user friendly towards the restaurant owners.

CONCLUSION

The primary reason behind the introduction of this online food delivery system is customers' comfortability, whereas the secondary factor is to build a platform for the expansion of business by the owners for attracting the user's attention, by permitting them to see the whole food menu in a single window with dish names, image, its specialty and price. The integration of a web food ordering system by the restaurants helps them to increase their sales, profit and corporate image. Restaurants consider these apps as a medium to approach their potential or target customers.

It can be concluded that, even though, the restaurants now serve the customers through online mode, it does not affect its direct delivery services. In order to serve the customers online, the restaurants incur service cost by way of commission to these online apps, which is compensated by the increment in sales and the profit thereby. Hence, the restaurants consider this online platform just as a channel to expand their business.

WORKS CITED

Tarun Varma, Krunal Tanna and Harshal Utekar (2018) "A survey on touch-based food ordering system in restaurants", International journal on recent and innovation trends in computing and communication, Volume-6, Issue-3

Jyothishman Das,(2011) "Consumer perception towards online food ordering and delivery

services", Journal of Management(JOM), Volume 5, Issue 5,

https://www.thehindubusinessline.com/companies/zomato-buys-ubereats-india-for- 206-million/article30979506.ece

https://www.swiggy.com

https://www.zomato.com

BIO-NOTE

Sejin Philip George is a B.Ed. Commerce graduate from Titus II Teachers College, Tiruvalla. He did his B.Com and M.Com at Christian College, Chengannur and Madras Christian College, Chennai respectively. His specialisation is in Commerce and Information Technology. He is a self-motivated person with sheer enthusiasm and determination.

CHAPTER XIV

IDENTITY, TRAUMA AND RECOVERY: PRISON BABY, A MEMOIR

Roshni Susan Varghese M. A., B. Ed.

ABSTRACT

Trauma can take an individual to extreme ends based on any past events that haunt them for a short period or in a long run. Through this research paper, the researcher tries to portray the traumatic phases faced by Deborah during her childhood and adulthood after knowing that she was born in a prison to a heroin addict mother. The paper also tries to emphasize her identity crisis as a black amidst the white and in her journey to find her roots.

Keywords: Prison trauma, race, identity crisis, traumatic phases.
Identity, Trauma and Recovery: *Prison Baby*, **A Memoi.**

• • •

INTRODUCTION

A memoir is a historical account or biography written from personal knowledge. It includes a collection of memories that an individual writes about moments or events, both public and private that took place in a person's life. It comes from the French word *mémoire,* which means "memory", or "reminiscence".

Prison Baby: a memoir by Deborah Jiang-Stein was published in 2014 by the Beacon Press, Boston, Massachusetts. The book explains the traumatic life of Deborah herself in twenty-six chapters. According to Merriam Webster Trauma is "a disordered psychic or behavioral state resulting from severe mental or emotional stress or physical injury".

Major objective of this study is to seek how the trauma of being an adopted child from prison, born to a heroin addict affects Deborah in her growth and shapes her identity as an individual as well as from the perspective of her race. It takes into consideration how trauma affected the life of Deborah from childhood to adulthood.

METHODOLOGY

For the in-depth analysis of the work, the researcher was able to learn about trauma and understand how trauma theory is emphasized in the book. In this paper, the researcher has used analytical approach to retrieve the imbibed data from the primary source and tried to find the relation of trauma theory throughout the work.

ANALYSIS

In the memoir *Prison Baby,* the protagonist, Deborah passed through many pains and struggles as a child and it affected her adulthood too. Her past always haunted her through different means. She had an identity crisis right from her childhood. From the beginning of the book, we can see that she had a great dilemma with her race as an adopted child. She always felt as 'the other' due to her caramel-colour in the adopted white family, class and neighborhood. She hated being amidst the white people and of not knowing her race. At home, she often got irritated with her mother trying to talk to her. She thought that her white mother is not able to understand her.

As a child, Deborah gets into her mother's room and there she discovers a hidden letter. She already knew that she was adopted so she suspected that the letter was about the details of her race, or races. But it was a letter which her mother writes to the family attorney requesting to alter Deborah's birth certificate from the Federal Women's Prison in Alderson, West Virginia, to Seattle. She also understands from the letter that her mother was a heroin addict and she lived in prison before foster care. This letter shattered her almost completely. It is from this point we can see the trauma of the protagonist become stronger.

I read the letter over and over, these new truths forever imprinted into my memory.

Prison?

Born in prison? No one's born in a prison.

The worst place, the worst of the worst: prison. And the worst people, from everything I've heard in cartoons and seen in magazines and heard from talk.

(Jiang-Stein 3)

Deborah was unable to accept the truth that she was born in a prison. She never imagined that she had such a past. Each word in the letter was carved into her brain. Her brain battled as she forced it to divorce from the reality, that she was born in a prison. Her thoughts of being born in prison began to haunt her. She realized that her "real" mother was an addict and a criminal and her "real" home was prison. She suffered the trauma of learning about her birth that leads her into a deep emotional lockdown behind a wall that imprisons her for the later twenty years.

The trauma of her inner consciousness made Deborah always see nightmares. Hallucinations and dreams are always part of trauma. Ernest Hartmann, states that dreaming is a way for the brain to work through trauma and dreams are often based on the emotion of a traumatized person experienced during their trauma. It is a time when they recollect this trauma (Hartmann 225). Her dreams made her to think about prison and her birth mother behind the prison bars. She saw this dream around every night and it haunted her.

"I wake up weepy, not fearful about the dream but, rather, sad about its recurrence, the repetition of images I can't understand." (Jiang-Stein 11)

Due to her trauma, she was not able to confirm to her surroundings. She doesn't know what reality was and what not reality was. When she plunged into memory, she began to make a relationship with her birth mother just in her thoughts. But this moved her away from her family and she hated her foster mother, who loved Deborah so much and she did not want to lose Deborah. But she ended up in her inner conflict of whom to love and she was not able to bring to a conclusion. She was not able to live in her present; she was haunted by her past. She was always in hallucination about her life.

Her early trauma made Deborah to cause a lack of strength to her thoughts. Childhood trauma in the first years over-stimulates and enlarges the amygdala, the part of the brain which processes emotion. This part of the brain controls impulses. The discovery of letter lead Deborah to a shock and the trauma pitched her into the tunnel of dissociative amnesia. To move from her traumatic thoughts, she acted very troublesome at school and everywhere she went. She tried to fade away the prison memories from her consciousness, but deep inside her it lied.

Her mental thoughts also affected her physical health which was common in most traumatic people. She often faced stress-related eating disorder. She felt hungry and wanted to eat her food, but the tightness in her gut forced her throat shut. She suffered from frequent stomachaches. Her mother and doctor just thought the stomachache was due to some bland food habits. But Deborah knew it was not food problem. It was concerned with the big prison secret. She thought about her prison life randomly and it made her physically upset.

"My gut's in a constant tangle and my mother drags me, trip after trip, to the doctor's office for my stomachaches. It's one of the random days I remember I was born in prison (13)".

It is clear that, the thought about her race does not leave her even when she grows up. When she joined a new college at Ohio, she was discriminated by the name of her colour. In truth there was no love big enough to cover the stigma and shame. Deborah carried about her prison roots or about her ambiguous racial complex. By the time her parents adopted her, no love was able to repair the trauma she had already lived or the traumas that followed her after that. She says that no one have ever told her that to which race she belonged to. She felt weird in this world because she has not seen anyone of brown colour with white parents. But she always tried to resist this thought through dance. She also loved music and learnt piano. Her favorite was Beethoven's "Moonlight Sonata". But even when she plays the keys it moves her to trauma.

"I tell myself, "A girl born in prison isn't supposed to play Bach or Beethoven duets with her mother." In the middle of a duet, I slide my stool back and take off to my room. Solitude was always my redeemer (34)."

When trauma affected deep, she tried new means and ways to make her mind stable. The traumatic stress and her inner conflicts later on took Deborah to drugs. It was in her seventh grade she started using drugs for the first time.

Within an hour I'm a 500-volt bulb, my every cell alive and at peace for first time. I need this forever. At last, I feel at home in my light-brown-yellow, don't-know-what-race-i-am-skin, my adopted-into-a-Jewish-family skin, my prison-born skin. Deep down, though, I still can't stand myself and am filed with hate for everyone. This rage and hate drive me to plan murder. Just in passing, but I give it more than a thought, and one afternoon in school, I sketch a plot with an older boy to off my parents. I plan to snake a hose from the furnace into their bedroom and gas them in the night. But if I kill them, where will I live? (48)

After using drugs, she turned into a stage in which she did not even think about her parents. She hated everyone around her. This stage was the most extreme and dangerous stage in her traumatic life. She was even ready to murder the people whom she hated. Every molecule of drug inside her packed her with rage. She felt that drugs gave her relief from all her problems. She was completely in another world without any tensions but only hatred for all people around her.

"When head and heart disconnect, the one thing left is total lockdown into a world of only two choices: adapt, or crash and fall. More often it's thought of as fight, flight, or freeze. I'm living in this zone full time (50)".

Deborah turned worst day by day and in her traumatic peak she tried for suicide. But her attempts got failed, even though she suffered a little pain. Later the only road she traveled was the self-destructive one. She started to bring out her frustrations and became more addictive. It was in her college that she smoked opium for the first time. She felt artsy instead of druggy. Later she was expelled from the college and then back in Seattle Deborah turned much more addicted. She moved with high dose of heroin and coke and felt a divine pleasure.

As the memoir progress we can see that a decade later, she turned her body into a drug-smuggling vessel. She used to fill her vagina with cocaine-filled balloons and trafficked across the border of Canada. She also craved out the inside of tampons and filled them with as much plastic wrapped coke and smuggle it across the border. If one of the balloons pops or the tampons leak then she absorbed enough coke to overdose herself. Along with her boyfriend Bobby, drugs became a living for Deborah.

She did not find any meaning for her life in the web of trauma. She turned out to be a professional drug smuggler and she just wanted all her prison memories to get buried under the essence of cocaine and heroin. She took all the risks in smuggling, even ready to give up her life. But it was not too late, Deborah stooped to ill health. When she was just turning nineteen, she was affected with an advance level of ulcer. Her light-brown skin and skinny body turned to much bonier due to too many drugs and due to the lack of nutrition for her body. She turned bony and fragile inside and out. But she did not have any attention to her and her health got worse. Later, she also began alcoholism.

As a traumatic girl when she became intense of drugs and alcohol she moved to sex. She moved through a series of romances and reckless sex with both men and women, where some relationships stood only for short a time. She didn't know how to be committed or how to stay in a relation because she never found anyone like loving them deeply. She even did not allow her family to love her. Her pre-adolescent sexual encounters also drove her further to more confusion, shame and secrecy. There came so many reasons for her to barricade herself in emotional isolation and it was another reason to dump her self-esteem down the drain, to doubt her worth. But born in prison was the primary concern it made her like such a victim of her growing trauma.

She turned out to be a full-blown addict. Even though she wished to leave behind this habit she was a failure. Deborah felt it completely impossible for her to drop out alcohol and drugs. She saw that all her peers have saved money and even started a family with their children. So, she purposefully made an attempt to overcome drugs and alcohol. But she could not and she went to a counselor for better help. She was emotionally still that twelve-year-old girl and the counselor told her that it was due to her experiences as an infant that turned her like that.

It was hard for me to believe this, but it sounds logical, even though the whole experience lives outside logic. She explains how what looked on the surface like bravado when I was a girl stems from a lack of impulse control, a problem that extended into adulthood because of developmental delays I experienced as an infant. She details how heroin babies go through withdrawal symptoms at birth, and they're bad, she says: convulsions, tremors, fever, sleep abnormalities and diarrhea. (73)

In various studies it is found that, half of the babies exposed to heroine are born dead and those who survive out of this are required great care to deal with the withdrawal and related developmental delays. Child welfare specialists say that something like ten percent of heroin infants have chromosome changes and six percent are born with neurological damage. The biggest problem for babies of heroin-addicted women is death. Specialists say since every drug a pregnant woman ingests passes from her bloodstream through the placenta to the fetus. Drug addiction in mother causes addiction for the baby too. After the birth, with the drug no longer available, a baby's central nervous system becomes overstimulated and causes withdrawal symptoms, which can even last from two to six months. It takes a lot of time to repair a traumatized brain of a child.

For Deborah it was the olfactory which was responsible for communicating into the amygdala and hippocampus. Both are part of limbic system, an area connected with memory and feeling, sometimes called the 'emotional brain'. It talks a lot about her past.

Deborah had a time of reflection of herself as such a baby, after talking to the counselor. Drugs were never social entertainment for her and alcohol was never just a beverage for her. They served as her anesthesia, a patch, a medicine, healing and freedom. Even it drove her to the biggest escape – death. Drugs ruined all her relationships and destroyed every corner of her life.

Later on, we can understand that, Deborah fell into depression and the she told her father and mother that she read the letter about her prison birth which gave her a great relief. As days passed due to her sickness and bad health she tried to strongly move away from alcohol and drugs. She began to recover herself.

In search of her past, she discovers that she has got a brother, Nick and understands more about her mother. She found that her mother was Greek, though she did not know her another half. She felt a wall crumble after her meet up with her birth mother's family. But even then, her past haunted her and she was not able to find a complete answer about her prison birth and herself. If people asked her what she was, then she had no answer to give them. She was in search of her identity. She felt like she was nowhere than fitting in too many places.

Even though she was a grownup she was not able to accept to the fact that she was born in a prison. She tried to ignore and push away her uncertainty about race and about her birth place, but then a feeling of isolation flooded inside her. All throughout her life it was the trauma of this prison and race that haunted her.

As an infant born in prison, Deborah felt prison as the first place she loved. But she just felt her existence as a meaningless one as a child born in prison. In secret, she always loved the word 'prison' and every word related to her first home such as dungeon, lockup, penal institution, detention center etc. but when she goes back to the prison for visit all her thoughts come back to her.

I can't believe I'm here, where I screamed the place down 24/ 7, spat out milk because my body craved her drug, the dope I'd grown with, plagued by withdrawal- vomiting and diarrhea. Like a dandelion puff of breeze, I fly off above the prison in a distortion of time and space, my cells dance. Did my mom's mind flip like this too? I fight emotional lockdown. I've no place inside where any of this fits. I'm at the threshold of something I've imagined my whole life. (90)

When she came to the prison for the visit, she moved into the thoughts of herself and her mother when they were in prison together. When she saw a hole in the prison the officer told her that it was the hole into which Deborah and her other went. Deborah says that doubt and distress and torment live in the hole, along with terror, frustration, boredom, rage, and depression.

She saw the hallway where her mother delivered her. Here senses were on fire, her cells were alive and she was without any words when she saw C7, the cell which she shared with her mother in that prison. It was the last place where her mother held and loved her. It was just a year that she spent her life with her mother. Her cell was her nursery and her bed was her cradle.

I turn and step into the door threshold, try to enter this five-by-eight-foot room, my first home. There's just enough space for a table, chair, and bed. I stand in the doorway and the cell soothes me like a scene in the dollhouse I played with as a girl. My home, this cell. I slept in here, ate, crawled around. My body melts, relaxes into a comfort like nowhere else before. (95)

After her visit when she was about to leave, the officer handed over an inmate bulletin typed on coarse beige newsprint, with a tow-inch sketch of a baby. Deborah realized that her original name was Madlyn Mary. Even though she knew her name, it felt as real for the first time. For the entire life she was waited for this moment.

She drove away from prison leaving the prison memories behind her. It was her greatest stigma and she did not feel like sharing it with the world. But for an interview Deborah was asked to share her story, but she felt that the stigma about her prison birthplace was like a terrain covered with cactus. The pain suffered by her mother haunted her too. She collected everything about her mother and her prison life, including Deborah's birth and life. The saga of Madlyn to Deborah.

It was a chance for Deborah to find herself. She realized that prison was not a place to raise a child. For a child the initial age develops them mentally. If they lose these initial ages then it would affect them tremendously. Torn from the love of her first twelve months she was unmoored and set to sail without any direction. The rage and anger Deborah expressed to her adoptive mother might be the feeling for her prison mother.

She knew why she had vomited on airplanes, and why the trapped diesel smell brought her nausea. It was an association from infancy, a conditioned response, even though Deborah loved travel and fly. Infants and toddlers gauge their environments by what the adults convey, and she traveled with a stranger, the federal marshal, about to enter void, the wide unknown, even worse than the void of the hole.

Deborah in her memoir also says that studies suggests that chronic intrauterine exposure to heroin causes hyperactivity, a brief attention span, and delayed cognitive, perceptive, and motor skills, as well as other developmental delays such as hypersensitivity to light, sound and touch. For Deborah as a girl, maybe it does explain the occasional pinball of language and sound inside me where at times it was too much for her to drive and talk at the same time. At another times, she says that sound and light bounce a battle for her attention during a group conversation.

The sense of smell often calls up powerful responses and memories in an instant from conditioned past experience. Infants who are exposed to drugs, alcohol, or cigarette smoke in the womb show a preference for these smells. These smells might upset another baby but for the initiated babies it would comfort them, like it comforted Deborah.

Babies who suffer from heroin and other drugs withdrawal also struggle with eating difficulties, overstimulation, and irritability. Deborah suffered PTSD, Post-Traumatic stress disorder, even from her infancy and later turned into RAD, reactive attachment disorder, in her adoption. This will affect a child and can permanently change a child's brain in development and hurt his or her ability to establish future relationships. Often caused by early separation from a birth mother, a child learns subconsciously it is dangerous to attach. RAD in children includes withdrawal from others, aggressive behavior towards peers, masked feelings of anger. They watch others closely but they do not get involved in social interaction and prefer to be all alone. Along with the prison trauma her racial identity made Deborah to make her life worse.

Deborah was ready to share her trauma with the inmates in prison because she wanted them to feel better. She used her life to show how we are all more than the sum of our parts and develop self- awareness among them. To overcome herself and to throw her haunted past, Deborah started public speaking through which she explored her purpose of life moving back her fears. She never felt alone after moving into her new life and now it is a hope for many people in prison trauma.

CONCLUSION

Based on the study and analysis, following findings have been made:

- Children born in prison have every possibility to lead a traumatic life and identity crisis emerges right from their birth and it develops within them gradually as they grow. It was evident throughout the childhood as well as adult life of Deborah.
- Prison trauma and realization of a drug-addicted or alcoholic mother may make people traumatic and even make them an addict in future. It may also lead them to various physical disabilities, drugs, alcohol, illegal sex and even suicidal tendency as Deborah faced.
- Trauma can affect an individual of not knowing one's root and race. It was what that made Deborah more traumatic.

WORKS CITED

Hartmann, Ernest, *Dreams and Nightmares: The New Theory on the Origins and Meaning of Dreams*. Basic Books, 1998.

Haupt, Jennifer. "Deborah Jiang-Stein: Staring down Stigma." *Psychology Today*, 25 March 2020.

Jiang-Stein, Deborah. Interview by Nerisha Penrose, ELLE, 17 May 2018.

Jiang-Stein, Deborah. *Prison Baby: A memoir.* Beacon press, 2014.

"Who Says The Past Must Define Us?" *You Tube*, uploaded by TEDx Talks, 18 Aug. 2015, https://www.youtube.com/watch?v=uvnZ0ApJg-c

"Women of Worth" *You Tube*, uploaded by Points of Light, 16 May. 2018,
https://www.youtube.com/watch?v=bqNSlxpv-uY

BIO-NOTE

Roshni Susan Varghese is a student of B. Ed. She has a Master Degree in English Language and Literature, and is very passionate to learn further in the field of Literature. She is interested to study more about the depiction of the human lives and their psychological situations in literary works. Her areas of interest are also related to Literature and other forms of art.

CHAPTER XV

TECHNOLOGY INTEGRATED PRACTICES FOR ENGLISH LANGUAGE TEACHING

Feba Susan BejoyM. A., B. Ed.

ABSTRACT

Technology has improved rapidly in recent years and this improvement is affecting the field of education. In this context, traditional educational methods have become inadequate as modern technology is also rapidly changing students' expectations and learning habits. In the post-covid era, students attending classes at schools are moreover distracted and disturbed and reluctant to be physically present in classrooms. Now-a-days, deep knowledge in technology is essential for teachers to effectively handle classes. As digital native students do prefer to learn in a technological environment, it is necessary and relevant to use different technologies to develop each of the skills in an educational environment. For the purpose of the study about integration of technology in English language teaching at the school level, in the initial phase, the researcher tries to focus on the identification of the main purpose of English Language Teaching. Then, the researcher categorizes the general purpose of language teaching and learning in the classroom. Finally, the researcher identifies and classifies technology integrated practices for each category. The research methodology adopted by the researcher is analytical methodology.

Keywords: Technology Integrated Practices, English Language Teaching and Language Skills.

Technology Integrated Practices for English Language Teaching.

* * *

INTRODUCTION

English as an international language is growing with time as it is an essential link language for interpersonal communication across the world, and is also essential for students as it broadens the students' minds, develops emotional skills and improves the quality of language usage. The importance of English language study has been well articulated in The National Curriculum Framework (2005) that English in India is a global language in a multilingual country.

In the post-covid era, students attending classes at schools are distracted and disturbed, and are reluctant to be physically present in the classroom and listen to the traditional way of teaching. Now-a- days, a deep knowledge in technology is essential for teachers to effectively handle classes. Using technology as a tool in classrooms helps both the teachers and the students in the following ways:

- Improves language teaching in students throughout their educational life.
- Engages students' productivity and creates active learners.
- Replaces the traditional monotonous teaching methods by the recent technologies
- To make teaching – learning process more interesting and worthy.
- Encourages individual growth and learning in students.
- Introduces new and innovative technologies to the students by using different technological resources so as to attain first hand experiences.
- To help the teachers in adapting classroom activities to enhance language learning.
- To identify the different technologies that can be used to teach each of the skills in English easily and effectively.

Technology Integration Practice is the process of using technologic tools in general content areas in education in order to allow students to apply computer and technology skills to learning and problem-solving. In this study, it means the recent and innovative technology (techniques, skills, devices, methods, processes or tools) used to transact information in English language classrooms. English Language Teaching is the practice and theory of learning and teaching English for the benefit of people whose first language is not English. This study focuses on teaching the skills of English Language in the Kerala syllabus schools.

Research objectives describe concisely what the researcher is trying to achieve through the research. Objectives can help the researcher to focus and narrow down the study to its essentials. The main objectives of the paper entitled 'Technology Integrated Practices for English Language Teaching' are:

- To identify the objectives of English Language Teaching in schools.
- To locate the various skills to be developed through ELT classes.
- To find out technology integrated practices for language classrooms.
- To categorise the technologies based on the purpose of teaching English.

METHODOLOGY

Methodology is the strategy or architectural design by which the researcher maps out an approach to problem-finding or problem-solving. For the present study, the phases through which the researcher would like to process are given below as the research design. For the purpose of the study about integration of technology in English language teaching at school level, in the initial phase, the researcher tries to focus on the identification of the main areas in English Language Teaching. For identifying the objectives, the sources from various sites in internet, textbooks and informal talks are depended. In the second phase, the researcher categorises the general purpose of language teaching and learning in the classroom. Finally, the researcher identifies and classifies technology integrated practices for each category. The research methodology adopted by the researcher is analytical methodology.

ANALYSIS

The present study deals with identifying the main aims of English Language Teaching, dividing it into five categories and allotting appropriate technologies that can be used (Table 2). The details are presented under the objectives of the study. The objectives are:

I. <u>**Purpose of English Language Teaching**</u>

From the data gathered from the secondary resources, the purposes identified in teaching the English language are highlighted in the table given below.

Purpose of English Language Teaching

Table 1 – Purpose of English Language Teaching

Sl. No	Purpose of English Language
1.	Developing Receptive Skills • Listening Skill • Reading Skill
2.	Developing Productive Skills • Speaking Skill • Writing Skill

<u>1. Developing Receptive Skills:</u> Receptive skills are the skills that a learner can receive and understand. The two receptive skills are listening and reading. These skills are sometimes known as passive skills. They can be contrasted with theproductive or active skills of speaking and writing. It deals with language development and retention: reading aids in improving grammar and vocabulary skills while listening aids in understanding a language better.

<u>2. Developing Productive Skills:</u> Speaking and writing skills are called productive skills. They are crucial as they give students the opportunity to practice real-life activities in the classroom. These two skills can be used as a 'barometer' to check how much the learners have learned. They are known as active skills as they develop the productivity of students.

II. **<u>Categorization of the Focus Areas</u>**

In order to strengthen the identified focus areas of English language teaching a categorization was essential.

Table 2- Details of the Categorisation of the Purpose

Sl. No	Purpose	Categorisation
1.	Developing Receptive (Listening and Reading) Skills	a) Developing Auditory Skills
		b) Promoting Silent Reading
		c) Encouraging Loud Reading
2.	Developing Productive (Speaking and Writing) Skills	a) Improving Communicative Skills
		b) Fostering Comprehensive Writing Skills

The purpose of teaching English is to assist the students to attain competency in using the basic skills of English, so that they can use it effectively and spontaneously at various situations. The general purpose of learning English can be categorised as following, for classifying the technologies appropriately for each skill:

1. <u>Developing Receptive (listening and reading) Skills</u>

a. <u>Developing auditory (listening) skills</u>

One of the basic skills in English language is auditory skill. According to Brett (1997), listening skill plays a vital role in language acquisition. Listening involves understanding the accent, pronunciations, intonation, meaning of words and meaning of speaking at the same time. It includes the ability to draw meaning from what is heard and to respond in action as a reaction to hearing.

a. <u>Promoting silent reading</u>

Silent reading improves students' understanding because it helps them to concentrate on reading rather than pronunciation. This practice also allows children to read faster and improve their comprehension. Silent reading also helps to develop reading skills for a purpose, as the focus is on understanding the content. This also helps students to retain thoughts into their subconscious mind and use them in their daily lives. Silent reading can increase comprehension, build vocabulary and improve writing skills. Silent reading provides the opportunity to learn the meanings of many new words in context.

c. <u>Encouraging loud reading</u>

Reading aloud is the foundation for literacy development. It is the single most important activity for successful reading. It builds important foundational skills, improves students' vocabulary, sharpens their focus and increases comprehension, provides a model of fluent, expressive reading, and helps children recognize what reading for pleasure is all about.

2. <u>Developing Productive (speaking and writing) Skills</u>

a. <u>Improving communicative (speaking) skills</u>

Speaking skill is the most important skill that the student should learn among all the four language skills in order to communicate with others and express thoughts and feelings. It helps the student to speak fluently, and correctly with proper intonation and pronunciation in the second language. A person can be a skillful communicator if he is competent in speaking fluently.

b. <u>Comprehensive writing skill</u>

Writing skill equips a person with communication and thinking skill. It also fosters the student's ability to explain and refine their ideas to others and themselves. Writing skills are an important part of communication where the students will learn grammar, spelling, punctuation, gestures, expressions used in writing, etc. It can sharpen creativity and imagination levels, widen the knowledge base and also increase the level of confidence in students.

I. **<u>Classifying Technology Integrated Practices for each Category</u>**

On the basis of the categories developed, the technologies can be classified as below.

Table 3 – Analysis and Classification of Technologies under each Category.

Developing Receptive (listening and reading) Skills

a.	Developing Auditory Skills	• Low- tech components
		- Radio broadcast, audiotapes, podcasts, tape recorders, IPODs, language labs
		• Mid – tech components
		- Films, videos, news, conversation, story narration, TED talks, video conferencing, seminars, lecture talks, PowerPoint slide presentation, Microsoft Teams
		• High –tech components
		- Apps (BBC Learning English, Learn English Podcasts)
		- Speech recognition software (Dragon Speech Recognition Solution, Google Docs Voice Typing, Briana, Speech notes, Gboard)
b.	Promoting Silent Reading	- Internet browsing
		- Multimedia software with subtitles (Windows Media Player, VLC media player)
		- Dictionaries and glossary
		- Textbooks, Newspapers/books, magazine, encyclopaedia
		- Reading-based computer programs (Prodigy English, Starfall, Storyline Online, ReadWorks, Oxford Owl)

c.	Encouraging Loud Reading	- Textbooks
		- Newspapers
		- Magazines
		- Encyclopaedia
		- Text-to-speech
		- Suggestopedia

Developing Productive (speaking and writing) Skills.

a.	Improving Communicati ve Skills	- Language laboratory, - Software (Internet Voice Chat) - Speech Synthesis Software (Alexa, Cortana, Google Assistant and Siri) - Artifical Intelligence (Lingvist, Duolingo, Gamification, Hello English, Memrise, Busuu, Lingbe) - Debates and discussions - Web-based storytelling - Phonetic transcript
b.	Foster Comprehensi ve Writing Skills	- Microsoft word - Blog - E-mail - Internet text chatting - E-portfolio - Writing articles, projects, action researchers, letters, applications, notices, description and accounts of events

I. Developing Receptive (listening and reading) Skills

a. Developing auditory (listening) skills

Multimedia technologies such as audio, video and animation are becoming commonplace and a potential tool for listening. The low - tech components (audio sources) like radio, broadcast, TV, audiotapes, podcasts, tape recorders, IPODs, language lab etc. are the most accessible ways by which a learner can develop listening skills. The mid – tech components (video sources) like films, videos, news, conversation, story narration, TED talks, video conferencing, seminars, lecture talks, PowerPoint slide presentation etc. can develop listening skills through which students will get to know about the language elements. High- tech components include all the computer technologies used to develop listening skills through apps like BBC Learning English, Learn English Podcasts etc, and speech recognition software like Google Docs Voice Typing, Braina, Speechnotes, Gboard etc. that can translate spoken words into text using closed captions to enable a person with hearing loss to understand what others are saying.

a. <u>Promoting silent reading</u>

Students can improve their silent reading skills with tools such as browsing the Internet, using multimedia softwares (Windows Media Player, VLC media player) with subtitles, using dictionaries and glossary, reading newspapers/books on the internet, and using reading-based computer programs. Reading-based computer programs, electronic glossaries and dictionaries increase students' vocabulary while the use of multimedia software provides motivation. On the other hand, reading magazines, newspapers, encyclopaedias, etc. (online and offline) can also, make a great contribution to the development of silent reading skills of students. In classrooms, teacher can ask the students to read their text silently or ask questions so that the students read it silently.

c. <u>Encouraging loud reading</u>

Teacher can ask the students to read the text or any other material aloud in the classroom. Newspapers, magazines or encyclopaedias in English brought to the class to support studies can be made to read aloud. Materials shown through PowerPoint slides are also helpful. Text-to-speech is computer-generated, and reading speed can usually be sped up or slowed down. Suggestopedia can be used to teach students to read the content aloud to familiarise the expressive language.

II. <u>Developing Productive (speaking and writing) Skills</u>

a. <u>Improving communicative (speaking) skills</u>

Language laboratories are influencing students' communication skills and speaking skills positively. With the help of softwares such as Internet voice chat and speech synthesis program (Google Assistant and Siri), ESL students can work on speaking. Internet voice chat programs are very useful in developing speaking skills and this program is a useful tool for students to have a chance to talk to native speakers anytime and anywhere.

On the other hand, artificial intelligence computer programs like Lingvist (Lingvist uses neural networks to assess students' existing vocabulary quickly and accurately), Duolingo (Produces apps for language-learning by which users can practice vocabulary, grammar, pronunciation and listening skills using spaced repetition), Gamification, Hello English (It allows users to learn the English language through interactive modules), Memrise (It is a British language platform that uses spaced repetition of flashcards to increase the rate of learning), Busuu (It is a language learning platform on web, iOS and Android that allows users to interact with native speakers), Lingbe (A free app to practice any language) etc. can improve speaking skills and such programs contribute to vocabulary as well as pronunciation.

In addition, it has been observed that the use of automatic voice recognition in mobile applications has improved pronunciation skills and increased motivation. Debates, discussions, web-based storytelling enhances student motivation, promotes creativity and imagination, and provides students with more opportunities to practice speaking. Phonetics can be taught in classes which can help students to develop proper pronunciation and speech. Internet, podcasts, video conferencing, videos and speech recognition software, etc. are considered the best tools for teaching speaking skill.

b. Comprehensive writing skill

Through Microsoft word, , ESL students can do italics, make underline, change colours, change font size, and even control spelling and grammar with the help of the program One of the popular tools that are widely adopted in the teaching of writing skills is blogs writer which provides a real-digital environment for communication. By writing via e-mail, social networks, and internet text chatting students can interact with someone else. The e-portfolio is an electronic archive that shows students' experiences, progress, and achievements and also includes writing studies written by them in the process. It helps students to reflect on their language skills and knowledge. Writing articles, projects, action research, letters, applications, notices, descriptions and accounts of events are also helpful.

CONCLUSION

The major findings that the researcher has identified through this study are:

- Both the receptive and productive skills are given equal importance for teaching English language at the school level.

Teachers have to introduce activities and technologies in English classrooms for developing and assessing receptive and productive skills along with their sub-skills. Technical opportunities are to be provided for students to focus and develop their productive skills rather than using traditional methods.

- Communicative skills can be developed at the school level by categorizing the main skills into sub-skills (Table 2).

Developing communicative skills at the school level is a basic necessity. Assimilation of skills can be incorporated by providing training and workshops for teachers. More research can be done in the field of developing technologies that support loud reading among students. English teachers must be aware of the latest innovative technologies and techniques available, which can be used for teaching each communicative skill separately or jointly in schools (Table 3).

Guidance should be provided to both teachers and students on the basis of technology. Teachers can use different technologies at a time, which can develop multiple skills in students. Technology-based games and apps can be used by teachers to support reading skills. Teachers can conduct Communicative English classes at schools with the help of technology. Technology-based- classroom arrangements can be facilitated in schools like language labs, smart classrooms etc. Teachers can give online home works, assignments, audio recordings, and presentations to the students so that they use digital technologies.

Based on the study, it is true to say that technology in the classroom provides teachers with more assistance and aids to support students. In addition to resources like textbooks and worksheets, technology equips educators with various tools to help students develop a better understanding of the material. For teaching different skills in language, teachers can rely on a variety of technologies as listed above for easy understanding.

This paper helped me to classify the technologies under each category which was identified on the basis of the purpose of teaching the English language at schools. The techniques that were listed can be used effectively by language teachers to develop communicative skills as a whole or by focusing on each skill. The incorporation of new and innovative techniques along with traditional methods can make the teaching-learning process livelier and more active.

WORKS CITED

'1.5 Technology Integration in English Language Teaching and Learning'. *PfDK MOOC Engelsk.* https://hiof.instructure.com/courses/4181/pages/1-dot-5-technology-integration-in-english-language-teaching-and-learning

'How to Use Technology in the Classroom: Benefits & Effects'. *Drexel University School of Education.* https://drexel.edu/soe/resources/student-teaching/advice/how-to-use-technology-in-the-classroom/

'Why is English Important for Students'. *Spears Language Labs.* https://www.languagelabsystem.com/why-is-english-important-for-students.html

Bloom, B.S. 'Taxonomy of Educational Objectives: The Classification of Educational Goals'. *Internet Achieves*. Longman, Green and Co. New York. 1956. https://archive.org/details/taxonomyofeducat0000unse_17x5/page/n7/mode/2up

Brett, P. "A Comparative Study of the Effects of the Use of Multimedia on Listening Comprehension." 1997.

Gunuc, Selim, Babacan, Nuri. 'Technology Integration in English Language Teaching and Learning'. Vol. 5. *The Journal of Teaching English for Specific and Academic Purposes*.

Mofareh, Alqahtani A. 'The Use of Technology in English Language Teaching'. *ResearchGate*.

National Curriculum Framework 2005. *National Council of Educational Research and Training*. 2 May 2005. https://ncert.nic.in/pdf/nc-framework/nf2005-english.pdf

Thompson, M. S. H, Wyatt, H.G (1952) 'Teaching of English in India'. Geoffrey Cumberlege Oxford University Press. *Internet Achieves*. https://archive.org/details/dli.ernet.503821/page/n1/mode/2up?q=Teaching+of+English+in+India

Vetriselvi. G. 'Aims and Objectives of Teaching English' *Language in India*. ISSN 1930- 2940, Vol. 16. 10 October 2016. http://www.languageinindia.com/oct2016/vertienglishobjectives2.pdf

BIO-NOTE

Feba Susan Bejoy is a Post- Graduate in English Language and Literature from Mahatma Gandhi University, Kottayam. She is an aspiring personality who has completed her B.Ed. course, and wishes to proceed further in making researches in new areas of language teaching.

CHAPTER XVI

LET'S REDEFINE, REINTERPRET AND REMAKE THE FAÇADE OF DISNEY PERSONAS

Adona Alexander M. A., B. Ed.

ABSTRACT

This paper tries to study how the modeling of Disney characters shapes and makes stereotypes in boys and girls. Disney personas often draw women as commodities; as an object for male gaze. The commodification of femininity (or 'selling gender') is a term used to describe how manufacturers strategically market products toward women to sell into and exploiting, their femininity and domesticity. Bandura says vicarious reinforcement occurs when an individual observes another person (a model) behave in a certain way and experience a consequence perceived as desirable by the observer, and as a result, the observer behaves as the model did. Aurora, Snow White, Ariel, Cinderella, and Jasmine, these personas are portrayed as beautiful, thin, fair, having apt physic for the pleasure of the heterosexual male viewer. The body structures of these Disney characters are designed according to the patriarchal framework. The plots of all these films are produced favoring the ideals of patriarchal ideology too. Focus is given more on domesticity, accommodating anything and everything according to what man likes and at the same disregards her interests, desires, and dreams. The study concentrates on outlining the impact of social media in gender formation, precisely the female Disney characters in the minds of children.

Keywords: Disney characters, gender Stereotyping, commodification and vicarious reinforcement

Let's Redefine, Reinterpret and Remake the Façade of Disney Personas.

• • •

INTRODUCTION

It is time to redefine, reinterpret, and remake the Disney characters for the next generation for the reason being children want to imitate them. Children are great imitators. Thus, from cradle to grave let them live a meaningful life designed for the better. Children watch Television, so more watching T.V. means more strong gender stereotypes instilled in them. Seeing the performances of Disney characters which are most appropriate for their age, little girls and boys believe in carrying them in the future. Stereotyping occurs when a person ascribes the collective characteristics associated with a particular group to every member of that group, discounting individual characteristics. Gender stereotyping plays an immense role in the upbringing of a child. Men are usually portrayed as independent, control freaks, and strenuous while women are personified as a dependent, emotional, and are at the mercy of others.

Gender behaviors are fashioned on the media model. Boys see superheroes strong enough to break down a building in one strike of fist and automatically in them there occurs instillation that they too should become one like them. Girls develop the same notion as they see Disney princesses or other female characters. They are stereotyped as being more fragile, soft, fair, amiable, and beautiful, accommodating, and do domestic work.

OBJECTIVES:

- To trace the adverse effect of gender stereotyping.
- To study the portrayal of women characters and its impact on little girls.
- To outline women as a commodity and the role of the male gaze.

METHODOLOGY:
<u>Analytical Research: -</u>

Analytical research is a specific type of research that involves critical thinking skills and the evaluation of facts and information relative to the research being conducted.

REDEFINING THE DEFINED

Little girls with dreams become women with vision. And it should be for the empowerment of the race as a whole. Disney personas often draw women as commodities. The commodification of femininity (or 'selling gender') is a term used to describe how manufacturers strategically market products toward women for the purpose of selling into, and exploiting, their femininity and domesticity. The study concentrates on outlining the impact of social media in gender formation, precisely the female Disney characters in the minds of children.

Vicarious reinforcement occurs when an individual observes another person (a model) behave in a certain way and experience a consequence perceived as desirable by the observer, and as a result, the observer behaves as the model did. For example, suppose a shy child at school observes another student being praised by the teacher for speaking up in class. The observed student is the reinforced model. If the shy child would like to be praised by the teacher and therefore personally speaks up in class in the future, vicarious reinforcement has occurred. Educators commonly use vicarious reinforcement to shape the behavior of students.

AURORA FROM SLEEPING BEAUTY:

The character Aurora from Sleeping beauty implies pretty girls do not even need to be alive to get some hot princely action. The story opens with the birth of a princess. Seven fairies are invited to be her godmothers, who all bless her with the gifts, the tools that a girl is supposed to get. Six of the fairies give the child various gifts: beauty, grace, dance, song, wit, and goodness. Why cannot she be gifted with books for knowledge, boldness for facing challenges in life, a protest for freedom, or the gift to be a public speaker or get to be what she wants to be? So, it reveals a girl getting gifts that are gender stereotyped, generally accepted by society. These gifts are given solely because it is believed to play a major role in her future life, right from hitting adolescents till the last breath or let us say as long as she is with him. Hyper femininity is the exaggeration of stereotyped behavior that is believed to be feminine. This may include being passive, naive, sexually inexperienced, soft, flirtatious, graceful, nurturing, and accepting. Princess Aurora gets all these hyperfeminine gifts from the fairies which adorn her life.

The old fairy however curses the child in retaliation for being forgotten. She proclaims that the child will one day prick her finger on a spinning wheel and die. The seventh fairy, who had not given her gift yet, attempts to reverse the curse, but she is only able to change a part of it. Instead of death, the princess will fall into a deep sleep that will last for one hundred years. She will be awakened by a kiss from the son of a king. What gibberish act is that? A girl is cursed and she is woken by the touch of a man and that too after hundred years of sleep? That can be a huge mistake of a model that any young girl can perceive. A girl child watching this will believe that the horoscope will change for the better as soon as a man enters her life. To all the girls out there you yourself have to rescue and no prince charming will aid out of the dark.

SNOW WHITE:

Beauty was the dominant curse for Snow White. Her own mother wishes that she had a daughter that had skin as white as snow, lips as red as blood and hair as black as ebony. The antagonist, the stepmother, wanted no woman to be more beautiful than her. So, she was a threat to Snow White but that same complexion was enough to gain a man. The motto of how a girl should be – 'fairest one of all' was the propaganda promoted through this very character. Snow White in order to escape from the evil woman wanders deeper into the forest and finds a small cottage that is the home to the Seven Dwarves. Seeing they are away; she dines on their food and falls asleep on a bed. The dwarves come back to a home in disarray and panic, assuming they have been burgled. They enter the bedroom upstairs and find Snow White, who explains her situation. They strike a deal, in which Snow White can live with them in exchange for housekeeping work. When Snow White lives she does everything to keep those Dwarfs happy. This apparently conveys that she is to satisfy their needs. Domesticity was the trade of this persona. She is truly safe as long as she does the chores of the home and keeps them contented.

Disguising herself as a hag, the wicked queen brings a poisoned apple to Snow White, who falls into a death-like sleep that can be broken only by a kiss from the prince. Again, man becomes the last resort. A handsome prince notices Snow White's coffin while out hunting. Remember they have never met before. And the kiss was given because of the physical beauty she possessed. Snow White immediately wakes up. Delighted to see that Snow White is alive, the prince professes his love to her. He proposes, and she agrees to marry him. They invite everyone in the land to their wedding, including the queen. Young girls should not fall for it. Life is beautiful with its curves and bends, ups and downs. But it is not as simple as the story of Snow White!

ARIEL FROM LITTLE MERMAID:

In 'Little Mermaid', the sixteen-year-old mermaid Ariel is dissatisfied with underwater life in the kingdom of Atlantica, a fantasy kingdom in the Atlantic Ocean. She is fascinated by the human world. Ariel falls in love with Eric, a human. A violent storm arrives, wrecking the ship, and knocking Eric overboard. Ariel rescues Eric and brings him to shore. She sings to him but leaves just as he regains consciousness to avoid being discovered. Fascinated by the memory of her voice, Eric vows to find the girl who saved and sang to him, and Ariel vows to find a way to join him in his world. Discovering a change in Ariel's behavior, Triton learns of her love for Eric.

Ursula makes a deal with Ariel to transform her into a human for three days in exchange for Ariel's voice, which Ursula puts in a nautilus shell. Within these three days, Ariel must receive the 'kiss of true love' from Eric. If Ariel gets Eric to kiss her, she will remain a human permanently. Otherwise, she will transform back into a mermaid and belong to Ursula. Ariel accepts and is then given human legs and taken to the surface by Flounder and Sebastian.

Eric finds Ariel on the beach and takes her to his castle, unaware that she is the one who had rescued him earlier. Ariel spends time with Eric, and at the end of the second day, they almost kiss but are thwarted by Flotsam and Jetsam. Angered at Ariel's close success, Ursula disguises herself as a beautiful young woman named Vanessa and appears onshore singing with Ariel's voice. Eric recognizes the song and, in her disguise, Ursula casts a hypnotic enchantment on Eric to make him forget about Ariel.

Ariel from 'Little Mermaid' portrays that it is okay to abandon your family, drastically change your body and give up your strongest talent in order to get your man. Once he sees your pretty face, only a witch's spell could draw his eyes away from you. Again, if you are beautiful enough, you could escape from the terrible conditions.

CINDERELLA:

With a wicked stepmother (Eleanor Audley) and two jealous stepsisters (Rhoda Williams, Lucille Bliss) who keep her enslaved and in rags, Cinderella (Ilene Woods) stands no chance of attending the royal ball. When her fairy godmother (Verna Felton) appears and magically transforms her reality into a dream come true, Cinderella enchants the handsome Prince Charming at the ball but must face the wrath of her enraged stepmother and sisters when the spell wears off at midnight. Cinderella, as a character, is the embodiment of modesty and diligence. She is a girl who has not lost her kindness even after her mother's death or after the cruelty from her stepmother and stepsisters. She tolerated everything patiently. Still, what changed her life was a rebellion, a violation of the rules. Although she was forbidden to go to the ball, she did it with the help of her fairy godmother. At the ball, she met Prince Charming who immediately fell in love with her. She was the only one in the kingdom who could win his heart.

'Cinderella' is a famous fairy tale that almost every child knows. It is a timeless story of the jealousy and innocence of a young girl mistreated by her stepmother and older stepsisters. This is the story that has won the hearts of many generations. By teaching children that being pretty and possessing the so-called feminine traits (fairer, good in domestic chores, accommodating, pleasing, etc.), will make them rise from the terrible situations they undergo, as soon as a man enters their life. Here, winning a man means the problems will be solved and the girl will become suddenly fortunate. And when you look for a man, do not forget to look for an affluent one. Looking good and being kind will not only be recognized but also rewarded. Just like how she fetched the prince. And the ending notion 'happily ever after'!

ALADDIN AND JASMINE:

Aladdin is a lovable street urchin who meets Princess Jasmine, the beautiful daughter of the sultan of Agrabah. While visiting her exotic palace, Aladdin stumbles upon a magic oil lamp that unleashes a powerful, wisecracking, larger-than-life genie. The oil lamp offers a change in the course of the young man's life. The young man who liked this lamp was more than what he seemed; a diamond, in the rough. Aladdin even the male character wants a drastic change economically. So that he can win the beautiful sweetheart, the princess. This story depicts the need to be financially sound so that a man can have a rich woman in his life. Here the children get the idea that whether you are a man or woman you should be or become rich. And consequently, the entire cosmos will stand by you, and then only your life becomes meaningful.

ADAPTING THE MASQUERADE

Vicarious reinforcement is a term popularized by Albert Bandura. One of his theories on the acquisition of behavior is vicarious reinforcement. Bandura also demonstrated that children could learn new patterns of behavior by observing other people without actually performing them or without the administration of external reinforcement. He referred to this phenomenon as vicarious reinforcement, which can be defined as learning through the observation of other people's behavior and seeing the consequences of such behavior. Three major determinants of vicarious reinforcement are one, the personality characteristics of the observer (such as gender, previous rewarding experience, etc.), two, the characteristics of the model (similar personal background, body structure, etc.), and three, reward and punishment associated with the model's behavior.

Through vicarious reinforcement, lasses imbibe the consequences of the behavior of these characters and then base or form perceptions and expectations on their gender role, they base a gender identity on these consequences and ultimately believe that is why they are created for. Women depend on men, waiting for a man, and as soon as a man approaches the whole unfortunate situation of the girl turns upside down. The tragic and disastrous horoscope changes with a man in the scene.

LEVERAGED DEMOISELLE PERSONAS

Gaze was a concept popularized by the British feminist film theorist Laura Mulvey to critique traditional representations of women in cinema, from which emerged the concept and the term of the male gaze. In feminist theory, the male gaze is the act of depicting women and the world, in the visual arts and literature, from a masculine, heterosexual perspective that presents and using Freud's thoughts, Mulvey insists on the idea that the images, characters, plots and stories, and dialogues in films are inadvertently built on the ideals of patriarchies, both within and beyond sexual contexts. It represents women as sexual objects for the pleasure of the heterosexual male viewer.

Aurora, Snow White, Ariel, Cinderella, and Jasmine, these personas are portrayed as beautiful, thin, fair, having apt physic for the pleasure of the heterosexual male viewer. The body structures of these Disney characters are designed according to the patriarchal framework. The plots of all these films are produced favoring the ideals of patriarchal ideology too. Focus is given more on domesticity, accommodating anything and everything according to what man likes and at the same disregards her interests, desires, and dreams.

SLAUGHTER THE STEREOTYPES

For young girls grow up watching these Disney films, it is all about being beautiful and fragile as that is the most important thing. That will get them a man and eventually get them out of trouble. So, what do Disney princes teach men about attracting women? Again, on the same boat. Generally, the same messages are fetched by the Disney princes and male characters too- be charming, be affluent, and be good-looking. Aladdin was charming and good-looking and he pretended to be rich to make Jasmine his. So here the projection is one of that what it is to be a girl, what it is to be a boy - the qualities needed to be successful. The Disney characters thus create typical girls and boys. This kind of vicarious learning and media exposure leads to the stereotyped narrow-minded generation. Children through them understand their own gender.

Non-stereotyping characters can change children's expectations at a young age. So, if little girls see a female doctor or female in the field as an athletic or female businesswoman through the characters, it can change their perspectives and expectations. They are not just seeing a stereotype; they think about it and conclude that they can also do those jobs. However, it was really found that some boys, the pre-teenage boys, when they were shown non-traditional models like a woman in a workplace, they actually displayed stronger stereotypes afterward as a reaction to it. So, when they saw females in the workplace or male nurses on T.V., they criticize it, they did not believe in it, they went stronger, that should be happening. Automatically they absorbed the notion that men should be doing this kind of job while women should do certain other types.

WORKS CITED

- "Parenting Quote / Kids Imitate Your Behavior: Parenting Quotes, Quotes for Kids, Kids and Parenting." Pinterest, https://in.pinterest.com/pin/524880531571427708/.
- "Sage Reference - Encyclopedia of Educational Psychology." SAGE Knowledge, 21 Apr. 2008, https://sk.sagepub.com/

reference/educationalpsychology/n276.xml.
- "What Is Analytical Research?" Reference, IAC Publishing, https://www.reference.com/business-finance/analytical-research-94534a536bf46028.
- "Male Gaze." Wikipedia, Wikimedia Foundation, 12 Oct. 2021, https://en.wikipedia.org/wiki/Male_gaze.
- Supersummary, https://www.supersummary.com/snow-white/summary/.
- Bondoc, Blythe. "'Little Girls with Dreams Become Women with Vision!'." Halos by Blythe, Halos by Blythe, 3 Jan. 2017, https://www.halosbyblythe.com/blog-archive/2016/12/18/little-girls-with-dreams-become-women-with-vision.
- Parenthood, Planned. "Gender Identity & Roles: Feminine Traits & Stereotypes." Planned Parenthood, https://www.plannedparenthood.org/learn/gender-identity/sex-gender-identity/what-are-gender-roles-and-stereotypes.
- "Snow White." Wikipedia, Wikimedia Foundation, 27 Sept. 2021, https://en.wikipedia.org/wiki/Snow_White#Plot.
- "The Little Mermaid (1989 Film)." Wikipedia, Wikimedia Foundation, 8 Oct. 2021, https://en.wikipedia.org/wiki/The_Little_Mermaid_(1989_film).
- TEDxTalks. "Stereotyping Gender - How Is This Still a Thing? | Linda Curika | Tedxriga." YouTube, YouTube, 15 Dec. 2016, https://www.youtube.com/watch?v=feX-aRtvdl0.
- "Laura Mulvey." Wikipedia, Wikimedia Foundation, 13 Dec. 2020.
- Varghese, George. A Study Book on Counselling. Christava Sahitya Samithi & TMA Institute of Counselling, Kottayam, 2014.

BIO-NOTE

Adona Alexander has completed Bachelors of Art in English Language and Literature at Marthoma College, Thiruvalla and has Masters in the same from Chengannur Christian College during the course of year 2017- 2019. She also holds a degree of Bachelor of

Education. Her interest areas range from Literature to Educational studies.

ARE WE MADE 'DISABLED' BY OUR OWN SOCIETY? AN ANALYSIS OF THE NOVEL MAHASHWETA THROUGH THE LENS OF DISABILITY STUDIES

Andria Joseph M. A., B. Ed.

ABSTRACT

The paper deals with the analysis of the novel *Mahashweta* by Sudha Murty in the point of view of Disability Studies. According to World Health Organisation, disability is not an attribute of an individual, but rather a complex collection of conditions, many of which are created by the social environments. Disability as the word suggests could be interpreted as a situation in which a person is deprived of his or her ability. As per the usual notion of the society the word disability is closely associated with an individual who is physically or mentally challenged. But on comprehending the word in a different perspective it seems to be associated with a normal human being as well. These are normally the disabilities attributed to an individual by the society on the basis of his or her caste, status, gender and so on. Disability is an umbrella term, covering impairments, activity limitations, and participation restrictions. An impairment is a problem in body function or structure; an activity limitation is a difficulty encountered by an individual in executing a task or action; while a participation restriction is a problem experienced by an individual in involvement in life situations. Disability is thus not just a health problem. It is a complex phenomenon, reflecting the interaction between features of a person's body and features of the society in which he or she lives. Overcoming the difficulties faced by people with disabilities requires interventions to remove environmental and social barriers.

Keywords: Gender Discrimination, Socio-economic status, and Chronic illness.

Are We Made 'Disabled' By Our Own Society? An Analysis of the Novel *Mahashweta* Through the Lens of Disability Studies

• • •

Sudha Murty, a prolific writer in English and Kannada, is most widely recognized as the head of the Infosys Foundation as well as the seed investor behind Infosys. The myriad experiences led her to be a prolific writer. Her writings are characterized by simplicity, minute observations, and wide knowledge of human behaviour. Her novel *Mahashweta* describes the difficulties faced by the protagonist, Anupama, after being affected by leukoderma. From the moment the world realizes that she is suffering from leukoderma, she is considered as a disabled person and is discriminated by the society. She was asked to move out of her husband's house and even had to suffer a lot in her own house. In an instance in the novel, she even attempts to commit suicide. But fortunately, she rethinks and decides to struggle hard to live. With the help of her friend, she manages a job as a lecturer in Bombay and emerges as an eminent personality inspite of suffering from leukoderma. The name 'Mahashweta' is taken from the female protagonist 'Mahashweta' in Bana Bhatta's play *Kadambari*. References also show that there is a very famous Marathi novel by Dr. Sumati Kshetramade with the same title and theme.

Disability studies is an academic discipline that examines and theorizes the social, political, cultural, and economic factors that define disability. Since the emergence of the disabled people's movement in the latter half of the twentieth century there has been a steady growth of interest in disability issues amongst social scientists in universities and colleges, referred to collectively as the 'academy' (Delanty) throughout the world. This has generated a radical critique of conventional thinking and research on disability related issues, a large and expanding literature from various "social sciences" perspectives, and the emergence of a new interdisciplinary area of enquiry generally known as 'Disability Studies'.

The description of disability studies adopted by the Society for Disability Studies comes perhaps as close as anything to an "official" definition of this new, interdisciplinary field of study: Disability studies recognizes that disability is a key aspect of human experience, and that disability has important political, social, and economic implications for society as a whole, including both disabled and non-disabled people. Still, despite such attempts at official definitions, it is probably not surprising that a certain messiness came to characterize the usage of the term "disability studies." It became somewhat unclear whether disability studies could be framed as a coherent and definable, if multidisciplinary, field of academic endeavor. As more and more academic programs began to spring up using the label of disability studies, disagreements began to emerge about who could and could not make legitimate use of the term. Some of the internationally recognized literary scholars specializing in disability studies are Michael Bérubé, G. Thomas Couser, Michael Davidson, Rosemarie Garland-Thomson, Cynthia Lewiecki - Wilson, Tobin Siebers.

"Disability is not an attribute of an individual, but rather a complex collection of conditions, many of which are created by the social environments" (WHO, p.28). Thus, disability could be analyzed on various grounds such as caste, economic background, gender, chronic illness and even in cases where disability of one person turns out to be a disability of the other. Disability studies, therefore, provides a vehicle to examine social attitudes, beliefs, and assumptions about disability as well as understand disability as a social and political category versus something to diagnose, identify, and label in individuals. It not only broadens the knowledge base about disability but also expands the epistemological boundaries of how this knowledge is produced. Scholars in disability studies believe strongly that the voice of individuals with disabilities is a necessity in the production of research and scholarly work and is central to the epistemology of disability. As a field, disability studies recognize and privilege the knowledge derived from the lived experiences of people with disabilities.

The novel *Mahashweta* is about the very homely and cheerful Anupama. After a fairy tale marriage to Anand, a wealthy doctor, against the wishes of his family, she faces unconcealed animosity in her new household as a poor daughter-in-law. As she braves against them, she is thrown into an abyss of cruel destiny when she discovers a white patch on her foot and learns that she has leukoderma. An insensitive husband obsessed with beauty, a resentful and uncaring family and the taboos of a narrow-minded indifferent society combine to break her spirit pushing her to the brink of suicide. In fact, her very own father rues, "Why did I have to father girls. They have become millstones around my neck" (72). However, the indomitable human spirit emerges victorious and Anupama rebuilds her life and career with great maturity of thought and action.

To live a life in this world for a human being means facing a lot of barriers, which in turn could be considered as the disabilities that society attributes to each one of them. This could be on the basis of his or her caste, gender, status, the disease that he or she possess or even on the basis of disability procured by others. Thus, the world turns out to be a place of hurdles where man has to race first, for being successful in life. The novel *Mahashweta* shows clear traces of these different levels of disabilities, where the female protagonist had to struggle hard, all alone, to face the hurdles in her life. Further, to a wider extent, even the experiences faced by the minor characters in the novel also shows elements of disability.

Caste is a form of social stratification characterized by endogamy and hereditary transmission of a lifestyle which often includes an occupation, ritual status in a hierarchy and customary social interaction and exclusion based on cultural notions of purity and pollution. Independent India has witnessed caste-related violence. Conventional marriages in India are usually arranged between individuals belonging to the same caste, religion, region, class, and culture. The marriage rules ensure that the basic cultural environment in which a girl functions after marriage is broadly familiar to her. Caste, as we know, exercises a greater corporate control on women than men in marriage arrangements.

The novel exhibits instances of caste discrimination. Being attracted by Anupama, Anand decides to enquire about her from Shrinath, Dr.Desai's brother – in – law. Their conversation reveals the importance of caste in marriage. "He knew that his mother was very keen on money, but as long as the girl belonged to the right community, she would come round" (23). It seems that marriage is a bond between two castes rather than being a bond between two minds. Thus, it may be concluded that belonging to a lower community or caste is considered as a disability by the society.

An individual's riches, not his or her looks, are most important if he or she wants to settle down, according to a pioneering study of the "marriage market" by psychologists. The same idea is reflected in the novel and this in turn could be considered as a case in which lower economic status seems to be a disability in the eyes of the society. In an instance in the novel where Anupama even though aware of her feelings for Anand decides to keep it aside realizing the difference in their financial backgrounds, the level of discrimination attributed to an individual on the basis of status by the society is revealed. "Given the difference in their backgrounds, she knew that it would be unrealistic on her part to dream of a life with Anand. She was the eldest daughter of a poor village schoolteacher, and destined to struggle her life. She was aware that Anand was favoured by Lakshmi, the goddess of wealth" (19). Her own thoughts reveal the notions of the society. "Reaching out for a star in the sky would only lead to disappointment" (19). This even shows the pitiful situation in which an individual has to accept himself or herself as disabled according to the mere notions set by the society and accordingly change his or her feelings.

The concept of lower economic status being a disability is even revealed through the perspectives of several minor characters in the novel. For instance, the criteria through which Radhakka,

Anand's mother, selects her daughter-in-law shows the importance of economic status, especially in the Indian context. "Anand wanted a beautiful bride; his mother wanted one who could match their status in the community" (21). Even the words of Sabakka, Anupama's step mother, contributes to the concept. "There is no comparison between their financial status and ours. Marriage should always be among equals" (28). The novel also brings in the pathetic situation of a poor father who is unable to conduct the marriage of his daughter in a manner befitting the status of her in-laws and thus he turns out to be a disabled.

"She was a practical woman and had realized that it would be impossible for Anupama's father to conduct the marriage in a manner befitting their status" (35). The novel even points out the idea that money is an important factor for us to be respected and it is revealed through the words of Girija, Anand's sister. "Just because you have married my brother, do not think you can tell me what to do. You should know your limitations" (44). Further, the piercing words of Radhika brings in the attention of the readers to the fact that money, a piece of paper, can even be considered as a mark to analyze a person's character. "No wonder they say you should check out the family background before you bring a girl into your home" (45). When Shamanna, Anupama's father, had sent her a hundred rupees, a large sum for him, by money order, Radhakka was disgusted. " 'The baksheesh I give our cook is more than this,' she muttered"(45). The novel also brings in instances where Anupama, the female protagonist, accepts the reality that she would never be accepted by her in- laws as she is not from a well-off family. "She preferred to suffer in silence as she knew that no one there was concerned about her" (46). If she had belonged to a well-off family, she would have been concerned and cared by her in- laws like a princess. But by fate she turned out to be the daughter of a poor village school teacher and is left to suffer in silence. Thus, the novel throws light to the fact that the phrase "money matters" really matters.

Gender discrimination is a term which means discrimination based on gender and it is only meant for women as females are only victims of gender discrimination. In India women are considered as pure, divine and worshiped. But on the other hand, she is discriminated against and victimized by the norms created by male dominant society. It is believed that in past (Vedic period) women had enjoyed equal status as men. The Upanishads and the Vedas have cited women sages and seers. But there also the practices like sati, jauhar, devdasis and purdah were prevalent. Then also there was a different role for both male and female in the society. This proves that gender discrimination is prevalent from that period and is still there. In India there is a diplomatic move against the women in the male dominant society as women are exploited by keeping her at a divine place and by worshiping her.

The novel also shows traces of gender discrimination. Perhaps in the initial setting of the novel the author brings in a trace of gender discrimination through the words of the nurse Prabhavathi. "Even though the female child is stronger than the male child at birth, as adults it is the man who becomes the oppressor, and the woman who suffers" (1). Later on, at an instance in the novel when Radhakka looks for the compatibility between the horoscopes of Anand and Anupama, the words of the family priest, Narayana seems to add to the idea of gender discrimination. "Oh, her horoscope shows only male children" (29). Moreover, through the sufferings of the female protagonist, Anupama, the novel also points out how things would be for a woman while the same situation would be different for a man. When her in laws realized that she was diseased she was even more harassed and tortured. She was blamed for ruining Anand's life. She along with her father was labeled as liars for they believed that she was diseased before the marriage and have deceived Anand and his family. "Oh! Are you sure it wasn't there before the marriage? Don't lie to me. Anand is far too naïve and you took advantage of him" (54). Everything would have been totally contrasting if Anand was the diseased person. Radhakka might advice Anupama to look after Anand as if it is the duty of an ideal wife to look after her diseased husband. She would even blame and consider fate as the culprit. Thus, Anupama turns out to be a victim of gender discrimination.

Another common level of disability faced by human being in a society is the situation in which he or she is diseased. Attitudinal barriers to ordinary activity are facts of life for people with disabilities. It is in the social construction of disability that we move from the particularity of any one disability toward the common social experiences of people with disabilities. Stigma, discrimination, and imputations of difference and inferiority are all parts of the social experience of disability. Being greeted at a party or a conference not by "hello" but by "do you need any help?" and having virtually every aspect of one's interests, tastes, and personality attributed to one's disability are also parts of the disability experience. Many nondisabled people assume that people with disabilities won't make good partners and cannot or should not become parents.

In the novel the author clearly brings in instances to reveal the pain that fate have inflicted upon the diseased. The thoughts of the doctor, described in the novel, clearly gives us an idea about the attitude of the society towards the diseased. "The doctor was aware that tiny white patches like that had ruined many marriages, shattered many hearts, broken many engagements. Most patients who learnt that they had leukoderma were overwhelmed by the social implications of their affliction" (49). The moment the society, especially her in-laws, get to know about her disease they reacted as if she had done a crime, although in this case fate is the real culprit. "All of them stood staring at the white patch on her foot... 'you wanted to expose me, but now you are exposed' "(53). The novel also shows how the dreams of a young married woman is shattered even before a bit of it is realized. At this instance of suffering and isolation even her husband ignores her for he gave much importance to her physical beauty rather than her inner beauty and it is evinced in the letters by Anand. "Anupama, I am busy coping with the workload at the hospital, but whenever I see anything beautiful, ..."(52). He was proud to own such a beautiful wife. Here Anupama seems to be reduced to an object, an object by the beauty of which its owner is proud. Thus, it seemed impossible for a person like Anand to accept her when she is being affected by a disease that damages her physical beauty. Here, his own words and promises to Anupama turns out to be meaningless. " 'Till death do us part...' And that is my promise to you. We shall always be together" (38). On the other hand, through the thoughts of Anupama the author makes us understand her faith in her husband. "'Anand is not like these people. He is a doctor. Surely, he will persuade his mother to see reason', Anupama told herself repeatedly" (56).

The words of the family priest, Narayana also shows how the diseased are restricted to take part in ordinary activities like a normal human being. "This is a bad disease. She cannot perform any puja now...Don't come in here and pollute everything" (54). She used to have her food with her mother-in-law but now food was sent to her room, implying their hesitation to give her company. Nobody cared of her or bothered to talk to her. Her position degraded to a level lower than that of a servant. Finally, she was asked to move out of her husband's house and her disability turned out to be a disaster in her life. "Take your daughter back with you; she need not come back until she's completely cured ..."(58). Moreover, in her own house she is left to suffer a lot. She had to face the harsh words of her stepmother as well as answer to the questions of the society. Further, through the thoughts of Anand, Sudha Murty points out the meaningless notion of the society by which the disabled are discriminated and those who are to be discriminated are encouraged and respected. "She had been shunned and abandoned only because of one white patch. On the other hand, Girija, who had had a sordid affair before her marriage, was held in high esteem in society and at home" (127). Even in Dr. Vasant's words, who happened to meet Anupama at the hospital when she met with an accident, there are traces of how the diseased are alienated and considered as disabled by the society. "People who have leukoderma feel like outcasts in our society because we look down upon them" (102). Finally, Anupama's own words shows the depth of pain that has being inflicted upon her mind when she questions Anand who has come to apologize for mercilessly betraying her as well as welcome her back to his life. "Was it my fault that I got this white patch?" (146). Thus, through these instances the author brings in the notion of the pain, isolation and deprivation faced by the diseased.

To a wider extent there are instances in which the disability of one person turns out to be a disability for another. The novel brings in this notion at an instance where the marriage proposal for Nanda, Anupama's step sister, has been broken because of the disease Anupama happened to procure. The prospective in-laws of Nanda fear that in the near future Nanda may also happen to procure the same disease, as in their view leukoderma is a hereditary disease. The letter from Nanda's perspective in-laws could be cited as an example. "We had heard a rumour that your eldest daughter has leukoderma and because of that her husband has left her...We do not want a daughter-in-law whose sister has white patches...Perhaps this alliance has not met with Lord Brahma's approval" (68). Even the words of Sabakka, which describes her fear of her daughters' future being ruined by Anupama's disease, points out the similar notion of the society and unfortunately it turns out to be a striking truth in the case of Nanda. "Once people find out that she has leukoderma, both my daughters' future will be at stake" (62).

Disability as the word suggests could be interpreted as a situation in which a person is deprived of his or her ability. As per the usual notion of the society the word disability is closely associated with an individual who is physically or mentally challenged. But on comprehending the word in a different perspective it seems to be associated with a normal human being as well. These are normally the disabilities attributed to an individual by the society on the basis of his or her caste, status, gender and so on. The author turns out to be successful in her attempt in generating awareness among her readers as at the end of the novel there is a description on how the novel happened to inspire a young man to marry a woman affected by leukoderma, whom he betrayed once when he came to know about her disease. Thus, it is proved that through the life of the female protagonist the novelist clearly depicts the different levels of disability as well as provides an awareness to the readers to consider the disabled. Moreover, the novel also depicts the idea of imperfectness through the poem recollected by Dr.Vasant, a character in the novel:

There is no perfection in anything in life.

Even in the great river Ganga there are black serpents.

The beautiful Saraswathi has jet-black curls;

The moon has a dark spot

Because even in nature perfection is not possible. (99)

WORKS CITED

Bhambhani, Meenu. "Narrativising Female Deprivation: The Disability of Singleness." *Gender and Narrative.* Ed. Jasbir Jain and Supriya Agarwal. Jaipur: Rawat Publications, 2002. N. pg. Print.

Colin, Barnes. "Disability Studies and the Academy: Past, present and Future." *Ars Vivendi Journal* (2011): n. pag. Mar. 2013. Web. 10 Dec. 2014. <http://www.ritsumei-arsvi.org/en/publications/read/id/4>.

Delanty, G. (2001) The University in the Knowledge Society. Buckingham: OpenUniversity Press. Web. 18 Dec. 2014.

"Disabilities." *World Health Organisation.* N.p., n.d. Web. 2 Dec. 2014. <http://www.who.int/topics/disabilities/en/>.

"Discrimination Against Women With Disabilities." *Second European Conference of Ministers Responsible for Integration Policies for People with Disabilities.* N.p., 7 May 2003. Web. 16 Dec. 2014. <http://www.coe.int/t/e/social_cohesion/soc-sp/confmin-iph(2003)6%20E.pdf>.

Ebi, Maliki Agnes. "Socio-Economic Status and Preferences in Marriage Partner Selection among University Undergraduates in South-South of Nigeria." Diss. Niger Delta U, 2011. Web. 16 Dec. 2014. <http://www.ajol.info/index.php/ejc/article/download/

72723/61639>.

"Feminity, narrative and Psychoanalysis." *Modern Criticism and Theory*. Ed. David and Nigel. 2nd ed. Singapore: Pearson Education, 1998. N. pag. Print.

Murty, Sudha.*Mahashweta*.New Delhi:Penguin Books,2007.Print.

BIO-NOTE

Andria Joseph holds her M. A. in English Language and Literature and her B. Ed. Degree in English Education from Mahatma Gandhi University, Kottayam. Her areas of interest include Indian English Literature, Gender Studies, Psychoanalytic Studies.

CHAPTER XVIII

ECOCIDAL IMAGINATION: A STUDY ON J.G. BALLARAD'S THE DROUGHT

Betsy Sebastian M. A., B. Ed.

ABSTRACT

Climate change is the defining issue of our time. One of the new genres of Anglophone fiction is the climate change novel often abbreviated as 'cli- fi', characterized by efforts to imagine the impact of drastic climate change on human life and perceptions. This paper attempts to analyse J. G Ballard's novel *The Drought* on the basis of Ecocriticism. The introduction of the paper presents the genre of climate fiction and sets J.G Ballard's novel *The Drought* as an example for this. A brief outline of the theory of Ecocriticism is given. The section titled 'Ecological Dystopia: Earth Burning Away and Society Falling Apart' focuses on the dystopian projection of nature in the novel explicating the havoc wrought by anthropocentric attitude.

The man-nature binary is deconstructed establishing the interconnectedness between human and environment through showing how the cataclysmic drought affect the residents. This chapter focuses on Barry Commoner's first law of ecology: "Everything is connected to everything else". The interconnection between nature and culture is exemplified through the impact of drought on human as well as nonhuman entities. The conclusion summarises the arguments stating the dystopian projection as a cautionary tale warning us of the perils of anthropocentric approach to nature.

Keywords: Ecology, Climate fiction, Dystopia, Ecocriticism, Anthropocene, and Anthropocentrism.

Ecocidal Imagination: A Study on J.G. Ballarad's *The Drought*

• • •

INTRODUCTION

Humanity's relationship with the environment goes all the way back to the early stages of creation in which the Holy Books framed human beings' relationship with the environment. The beginning of the first book of Bible has often been regarded as the origin of God's dictate on man to master and subjugate all living forms on earth for he is labelled as the crown of creation. Eco-criticism is the study of literature and environment where scholars analyse and interpret the literary projection of nature and environmental issues in a literary text. Eco-criticism is also known by a number of other designations including, 'green (cultural) studies', 'ecopoetic' and 'environmental literary criticism'. "Ecocriticism designates the critical writings which explore the relations between literature and the biological and physical environment, conducted with an acute awareness of the damage being wrought on that environment by human activities" (Abrams, 96). Ecocriticism is the study of the relationship between literature and the physical environment... ecocriticism takes an earth-centered approach to literary studies. (Glotfelty xviii)

Anthropocentrism is defined as the view which places the human perspective of nature at the centre of all thought. It is largely based on human-centeredness and sets the human perception as the dominant norm. One of the major goals in ecocriticism is to study how individuals in society behave and react in relation to nature and ecological aspects. Arne Naess's notion of Deep Ecology emphasizes a holistic world view stressing the interconnectedness of all life forms and natural features. Deep ecology takes a firm stand against anthropocentrism and it asserts that we need to change our view from anthropocentrism to ecocentrism. All ecological criticism shares the fundamental premise that human culture is connected to the physical world, affecting it and affected by it.

J. G. Ballard is one of the most influential Science Fiction writers belonging to New- wave. Ballard's unique perspective of modernity has not only earned him the title 'Ballardian'. This adjective is coined to describe the situations like man-made and bleak. A significant quality of The Drought is the very fact that the cataclysm is fully anthropogenic. In *The Dought*, it is drought which creates shortage of water and consequential threat of extinction of entire humanity novels is the intention of an author to convey a message that human habit of over use of natural resources and his indifferent behaviour towards the natural cycle would become the main reason of self-destruction in near future. The problem now, as most ecologists agree, is to find ways of keeping the human community from destroying the natural community, and with it the human community. This is what ecologists like to call the self-destructive or suicidal motive that is inherent in our prevailing and paradoxical attitude toward nature. The conceptual and practical problem is to find the grounds upon which the two communities-the human, the natural- can coexist, cooperate, and flourish in the biosphere.

The novel envisions environmental apocalypse as it explores a portrayal of endangered human race due to crushing heat and endless quest for water. Ballard focused more on 'inner space' than 'outer space'. In other words, he merges the physical with the psychological and the body with the soul in order for a homogeneous self and society. This paper attempts to explore The Drought in terms of ecological dystopia regarding the relationship between nature and humankind. To this end, ecocritical theory will be employed to expose how humanity affects and is affected by nature during a ten-year drought in Larchmont, a lakeside town on the eastern coast of America.

ECOLOGICAL DYSTOPIA: EARTH BURNING AWAY AND SOCIETY FALLING APART

Focusing on the theme of climate change, Ballard's novel serves as a mental laboratory that stimulates the potential consequences of climate change. Ballard expounded that his novel The Drought represents a future dominated by sand, which becomes the end of the world. The novel, as the title implies, depicts a world threatened by drastic climate changes caused by heavy industrial activities.

The novel instantly begins in a cataclysmic setting: "At noon, when Dr. Charles Ransom moored his houseboat in the entrance to the river, he saw Quilter... smiling at the dead birds floating in the water below his feet. The caking mud bank was speckled with pieces of paper and driftwood" (5).

The setting of *The Drought* represents ecological changes where we see the discursively manipulated nonhuman world. The author delineates how landscape changes over time and how these changes influence the human psyche. Ballard shows how the river has gone dry by illustrating the river before and after the drought:

The lake, once a clear stretch of open water thirty miles in length, had subsided into a series of small pools and channels, separated by the banks of draining mud... Normally, at late summer, the river would have been almost three hundred feet wide, but it was now less than half this, an evil-smelling creek that wound its way along the flat gutter of the banks (56).

Ballard sets the setting of the novel by depicting the vast changes that have taken place in the natural environment. The absence of water immediately affects animals such as birds and fish that begin to die out. The dead fish and bird body imagery foreshadow the death of

humanity. As they approach Larchmont anyway, Ransom feels that they are entering a graveyard.

Nature in the novel is extraneous to the Real, though often it evokes nostalgia and a sense of exile, for the planet itself no longer feels like home to a number of characters. Nature is no longer a central presence in the world of the novel, no longer the life-sustaining air. Ballard does not abstain from mentioning the good old days when life and nature were at their best condition when: "What was once a vast pond of open water has transformed into stiff banks of mud" (29). The bed of the lake, almost drained, formed an inland beach of white dunes. In an interview, Ballard mentioned that:

In my novel *The Drought*, I see the future as a world dominated by sand. It is the end of the planet, and the few people who survive on the planet are governed by perfectly abstract relations. It is a completely abstract world, as abstract as the most abstract of painters or sculptors one can imagine. (Sellars 12)

Ballard reflects a clear portrait of doom and destruction. This image of blind nature is created and visually depicted by Ballard so as to set the scene of a major, ecological disaster. It is worth noting that the author not only designates the decay of the physical environment but also of all non-human living beings. The dead birds and the drying fish foreshadow the dying condition of Earth and the similar bleak future that awaits humans.

In the novel, nature is presented as hybrid- transformed by human intervention and technology- but also as sick, dying, destroyed, and as something lost, absent, mourned and virtually only remembered in dreams. The distant dream is given as: "Rain! – at the recollection of what the term had once meant" (13). The Drought re-imagines nature, re-contextualizes environments, and ultimately presents post-natural world pointing out the possible tragic consequences of the failure to overcome environmental issues in our time.

.Ecocriticism sees the devastation of earth as the result of human behaviour such as exploitation of the environment. The issue of devastation of earth becomes the centre point of interest which grasps the whole setting of the novel. It portrays the colourless world because of devastation. The city is changed into "a wasteland of dust and ruined towns" (147). The devastation forebodes the apocalypse that it shows total destruction or absence of future. "There can't be much future for them there" (51). The same on the other hand signifies the use and throw, consumerist attitude where nature is seen as creation to serve humans. The cetrality of the human over the natural ensures the exploitation of the latter.

Emphasizing the cultural as well as scientific aspects of climate change, he concludes that the current global crisis has occurred 'not because of how ecosystems function but rather because of how our ethical systems function'. Rapid industrial growth and environmental loss appears as cause and effect in the novel. The self-destructive or suicidal motive that is inherent in our prevailing and paradoxical attitude toward nature. The imbalance and the consecutive effects are purely human creations and this presents the drastic effect of anthropocentric attitude to nature. So, this ecocidal human activity turns out to be homicidal.

Dystopias portraying environmental collapse due to human meddling portray their ecocriticism by exploring the relationship between human and nature. In order to observe those processes of change that affect the relationship, ecologists study the mutual effects that other species, natural forces, and cycles have on humans, and the actions of humans that affect the web of connections with non-human organisms and entities. "Ecological criticism shares the fundamental premise that human culture is connected to the physical world, affecting it and affected by it". (Glotfelty xix).

In *The Drought* we see a handful of characters who are in harmony with nature like the fisher folk, Philip Jordan and Charles Ransom. The fishermen prove to live close to nature. Philip Jordan who is presented as the "foster child of the river" rescuing a swan which was found "suffocating in the oil" (26). Ransom and Catherine Austen attempts to feed and water the animals in the zoo though they are hopeless to keep them alive by Lomax, indicating "the dusty villas along the river", tells Ransom "[t]hey look like mud huts already. We're moving straight back into the past" (31). Ballard tried to show that human beings are affected by the changing world so much as they transform the planet into a devastated land. The more the river dries up, the more it destroys the communities of fishermen whose lives are maintained by its flow, and thus every individual falls apart from the society and gets lost in time.

Modern existence can be related as homo clausus, a kind of modern false consciousness intent on ignoring the fundamental necessity of social interdependence. Literally the 'closed personality' of modern human subjectivity. Homo clausus represents a model of the modern self is essentially unaware of its necessary, substantive connectedness to others. He insulates himself from his surrounding environment inviting self-destruction. This is an individual who is typically even less conscious of the long histories of human interdependency that are constitutive of modern subjectivity.

Towards the end of *The Drought*, all the characters set out in an expedition to find water. They migrate towards the shore in search of water to sustain their life. The desert Odyssey is in fact a quest for existence. It is worth mentioning here that the tradition of earning a living for the family also changes with the drought in the way that breadwinning is transformed into getting water. As suggested previously, the concept of time becomes meaningless on the coast this time because people are disconnected from their past; their memories have faded away for the sake of survival; and the world is stripped away of meaning and value:

This eco-catastrophe is framed as an act of 'retribution by the sea' nature's response to human beings' use of cetyl alcohol films, which prevent evaporation from water reservoirs. Waste, in this context, is not merely a manifestation of physical devastation and social unrest, but the matter from which the future itself will be composed. Navigating the future will involve making sense of these "unresolved residues of the past" (152).

Humanity, being at the mercy of the nonhuman world, strives to survive in the parching land by murdering and stealing under such bitter conditions. Ballard evinces that destruction of the natural world corrupts the human spirit more and more, which can be cited by the fight between the fishermen and the churchmen when the former group burn churches and the latter group set fire to some houses in the town.

In *The Drought*, the protagonist is forced to deliberate on his relationship with nature; forced to redefine the human condition. The discrepancy found in aiming to understand individual responsibility in the realisation of the 'hyper object' of global warming.

One of the basic formulations of ecology is that there is a one way flow of energy through a system but that materials circulate or are recycled and can be used over and over. But in The Drought the water cycle is broken causing the cataclysm. As the natural water cycle is disrupted by a polymeric film covering major ocean surfaces- caused by industrial pollution- the resulting drought is exacerbated by an atmosphere suffused with smog and dust columns. Barry Commoner's first law of ecology, "Everything is connected to everything else" (Glotfelty xix) forms the basis on human nature inter connectedness. This need to see even the smallest, most remote part in relation to a very large whole is the central intellectual action required by ecology and of an ecological vision. It is a vision that human life is "conjoined" with the life of nature. The biosphere (or ecosphere) is the home that life has built for itself on the planet's outer surface and there is a reciprocal interdependence of one life process upon another, and there is a mutual interconnected development from of the earth's life systems. Critiquing the binary of man/ nature the mutually exclusive oppositions are subverted into interconnectedness and we see that human experience of the natural environment is mediated by culture.

Thus, human relations are vital in understanding the ecological crisis. Human mentality of being aggressively competitive and dominant towards one another has resulted in humanity's ruthless domination of nature. Moreover, the cruel competitive capitalist spirit, which masses have taken for granted, is responsible for the rising environmental imbalance which is posing a serious threat to our planet. In order to establish a nature-friendly spirit, a complete abolition of hierarchy is necessary.

At the end of The Drought, various characters seem to lose their sense of reality and transcend into the sub-conscious domain. The characters are not just bizarre but also haunted and controlled by technological, urban aspects that represent the former capitalist world order. It seems clear that Ballard's post- capitalist, new world order is ambiguous, obscure and meaningless (Firsching 305).

Ballard's ending of *The Drought* is bleak but again quite ambiguous as the author reveals signs of recovery in ecological terms. In an unexplained manner, the sun recedes into the sky, the climate becomes cooler and eventually rain starts dropping from the air. Despite the destruction of a great many living beings including humans and various animals, nature is in a process of restoring and renewing herself. Without any human interference, nature is now free at last.

Bookchin's notion of free nature manifests itself at the very end of the novel as the one and only solution for the salvation of nature.

CONCLUSION

J. G Ballard's *The Drought* critically shows that how man selfishly destroying his natural world and endangered his existence along with all other species. The novel discloses that environmental catastrophe does not happen overnight, which means it takes a while to reach its apocalyptic level. The novel discusses that humanity is gone under such calamitous circumstances because people are alienated to themselves and to each other and they become hostile towards the others for survival.

The Drought also reflects ecological consciousness as the author has extended the real environmental problems in his fictional world that mirrors the futuristic scene of the world. The delineation of characters represents entire humanity and he was not describing the future but the present. Climate Fictions use post-apocalyptic, dystopian, ecological forms and also provide solutions to environmental imbalance which intensifies the sensibility of reader. So the first chapter explicates the havoc wrought by anthropocentric attitude. The post natural novum is undesirable for human existence.

Novels which are informed by a 'toxic consciousness' as political texts: insomuch as they provide representations of a postnatural world, of a culture defined by its waste, and of a nation that has fouled its own nest, these novels do much to raise the environmental consciousness of the society that sees itself in the mirror. As given in the first chapter in The Drought we see a world threatened by drastic climate changes caused by heavy industrial activities as is about to bring the end of civilization. The Drought is a Ballardian reflection of humanity's bleak future clear portrait of doom and destruction. Ecocriticism sees the devastation of earth as the result of humans' behaviour such as exploitation of the environment. Dystopian projection impels the conviction that what is at stake is not only the well- being but, ultimately the survival of human life.

Ecological criticism shares the fundamental premise that human culture is connected to the physical world, affecting it and affected by it. The drought forces the residents of New Hamilton to the desert. The ecological calamity brings forth the irrationality in him causing feuds, skirmishes and shooting. Water becomes so costly that thieving it becomes the severest crime. So a clear acceptance, rather than dominion, will help us to live peacefully. Opposed to the anthropocentric view we should embrace an eco-centric view for our existence is closely tied with nature.

Social ecology parallels hierarchy in society as the cause of man's domination over nature. Hierarchy and the mentality resulting from it is one of the true reasons that causes all forms of oppression and leads to exploitation. In Bookchins view, we should, the two natures, primary or biotic nature, and second or social nature, are interrelated and influences each other. In other words social relationship with one another is directly responsible for the outcome of the nonhuman world. Rather than a hierarchical relation we should coexist with each other as well as with nature.

Most ecocritical work shares a common motivation: the troubling awareness that we have reached the age of environmental limits, a time when the consequences of human actions are damaging the planet's basic life support systems. Following McHarg and rephrasing a fine old adage, we can say that "where there is no ecological vision, the people will perish." And this ecological vision must penetrate the economic, political, social, and technological visions of our time, and radicalize them. The problem is not national, but global, planetary.

WORKS CITED

Ballard, J. G. The Drought. Fourth Estate, 1965.

Firsching, L. J., & P, R. M. (1985). J.G. Ballard's Ambiguous Apocalypse. Science Fiction

Studies, 12(3), 297-310. Retrieved from https://www.jstor.org/stable/4239704, P. 305 Fromm, Harold. "From Transcendence to Obsolescence: A Route Map" PP.30,39

Glotfelty, Cheryl. The Ecocriticism Reader: Landmarks in Literary Ecology, edited by Harolf

Fromm, The University of Georgia Press, 1966, p. xix

Glotfelty , Cheryll and Harold Fromm.Landmarks in Literary Ecology.. Athens: U of

Georgia, PP. 225,40.

Sellars, S., & Hara, D. O. (2012). Extreme Metaphors Selected Interviews with J.G. Ballard.

London: Fourth Estate, P.12.

BIO-NOTE

Betsy Sebastian is a post graduate in English Language and Literature. She holds her Bachelors Degree in Education from Mahatma Gandhi University, Kottayam. Her areas of interest include Poetry, Literary Theory and Cultural Studies.